UNBROKEN VESSEL

One little girl's story of survival and her determination
to become a woman of beauty and hope…

My Brother "Chickie" (Frank Mileti) and I.

A MEMOIR

ELAINE GORDON

Elaine Gordon

To contact the publisher, visit www.kdp.amazon.com

To contact the author, visit www.elainegordonconsulting.com

ISBN: 978-0-578-47909-5
eBook ISBN 978-0-578-48284-2

First printing: March 20, 2019

Cover design: Ernie Sanchez
Cover concept: Elaine Gordon
Cover photo: Dav Anmed
Cover styling: Estella Flores
Back cover photo: Dav Anmed
Editor: Kim North
Creative Assistant: Howard Baumaister

Published by: Kindle Direct Press

Printed in the United States of America

First Edition

UNBROKEN VESSEL

SURVIVED CHILDHOOD

SURVIVED ADOLESENCE

SURVIVED TO CONTINUE ...

- Elaine Gordon

Elaine Gordon

UNBROKEN VESSEL

"You are not defined by what happened to you — you are defined by what you do with what happened to you"

\- Elaine Gordon

"Health is your greatest wealth. If you have your health, you have everything"

\- Marie Mileti, my mom

Elaine Gordon

UNBROKEN VESSEL

"NEVER, NEVER, NEVER, GIVE UP"

- Winston Churchill

DEDICATION

My late mother, Marie Mileti

My brother, Frank Mileti

My daughter, Shavawn Gordon-Rissman

DEDICATION

MY LATE MOM, MARIE MILETI –

To my beautiful mother, whom I miss every day. Thank you for teaching me how to love and forgive all those that hurt me. I especially appreciate how much you truly loved me and did the best job you knew how in raising my brother and me. I am most appreciative for the soft heart that you helped develop in me so that I could have the same love you have me for others, especially the poor. I am the woman today, mom, because of you.

MY BROTHER, FRANK MILETI (AKA-CHICKIE) –

There is no doubt in my mind that my brother is one of the closest people on earth to me. My love goes beyond all of the fights we got into—that I won—until my brother grew bigger than I did. I also appreciate how much he protected me and tag-teamed with me for the first 18 years of our lives. The best part of my relationship with my brother is that he has been the greatest inspiration and gift to me. I would not have had this book authenticated had he not put in long hours pre-editing my rough manuscript before it was sent to the editor. However, I did have a hard time with him writing his own continued story into my story. For the extra contribution that he added, I was lovingly compelled to delete his input. In turn, I cordially encouraged him to write his own book! Thank you, bro, for loving me, always having my back, and for waiting for me so that I could catch up to you in age every year.

MY DAUGHTER, SHAVAWN GORDON-RISSMAN –
God in His great grace and glory blessed me with the privilege of raising an amazingly beautiful, talented and loving daughter. She was my first real-life experience of parenting a child and my first involvement actually holding an infant. I think I was more afraid of her than she was of me when I brought her home from the hospital. We both had a big learning curve to bridge as far as this parent-child thing. She was the driving force in my life that caused me to make something of myself. She gave me the will power and the joy to get up every morning and become the best mother I could be. My daughter, Shavawn, has grown into such a beautiful woman that words can't express the pride and admiration I have for her. Out of all my suffering and pain, God replaced my mother in my life with a little girl who would continue loving me unconditionally. For that very reason, I could go on. The challenges I faced raising her essentially by myself, not married, gave me great strength and hope for a better future for us. Thank you Shavawn, for always being there for me, even though I believe my mother's predictions came true. My mom would constantly remind me that I would give birth to a daughter just like me. I am convinced that she is somewhat of a milder version of me—strong-willed, determined and she definitely tries to parent me. I basically remind her that I gave birth to her, so I am in charge!

MY SONS, PAUL MICHAEL GORDON
AND JONATHAN DAVID GORDON,
(AKA-AIRSHIP ENOCH) –
Both of you boys had not been born yet at this point in my memoirs, so please don't feel left out, because book two will definitely be about both of you! On another note, what a wonderful addition you both were to me, and this story will be told at another time.

TO OTHERS IN THIS STORY AND WHO WERE RESPONSIBLE FOR MAKING THIS BOOK POSSIBLE, YOU WILL BE MENTIONED IN MY ACKNOWLEDGEMENTS. THANK YOU FOR ADDING SUCH BEAUTY TO MY LIFE.

Elaine Gordon

TABLE OF CONTENTS

Elaine Gordon

REVIEWS FOR UNBROKEN VESSEL

The many accounts throughout the pages of "Unbroken Vessel," share Elaine Gordon's inspirational and riveting, true story of her perilous life growing up in an unsafe world living in the welfare housing projects of New York City's Lower East Side. Through a series of anecdotes, she recounts the events that impacted and molded her life. Rather than allowing adversity to defeat her, the love and support of her ill-health mother helped her to learn the lessons to become a stronger and more successful individual.

"Unbroken Vessel" is a heartwarming and uplifting book that reminds us all that a person is not only characterized by their experiences, but how they react to and use those experiences to grow as a person.

- Ted Bujewski, Senior Dept. of Defense Official

Life is all about choices, experiences and people and the symbiotic relationship between the three. The argument over nature vs. nurture leads one to question why two people from similar backgrounds and experiences can end up leading lives so different from each other.

In "Unbroken Vessel" we encounter the harrowing experiences by Elaine Gordon growing up in the "slums" of New York City. Her powerful and poignant misadventures at such a young age resonate with even those of us who were never introduced to "street culture."

We are all exposed to fear, death, loss, failure and the consequences of bad choices. Some of us to greater degrees than others, but the experiences are still never lessened.

As I read through the pages of "Unbroken Vessel" and Elaine Gordon's journey through her heartbreaks and joys, I was moved and empowered by her resilience. This is something we can all learn from at any age.

- Pat Smith, CHHC- alumni graduate of IIN

Elaine Gordon writes in a very carefree style that is easy to digest and is also very entertaining. "Unbroken Vessel" presents the flavor of the inner New York City lifestyle, only experienced by just a few. I can relate very well with this background as I grew up in the South Bronx, also by a single mother.

The book presents an interesting set of characters that touch and influence Gordon's life. It is said, we are all a product of our environment and how that molds our lives. Knowing Elaine Mileti Gordon personally, I can certainly see how the events described in, "Unbroken Vessel, have shaped her to rise above and escape poverty through hard work and fortitude.

One can only wait with excitement and anticipation for the sequel of the compelling and page-turning books to follow.

- Howard Baumaister, Former S.V.P. of City Bank, NYC

"The miraculous true story of a woman who took the broken pieces of her life and put them back together. Life should never have to be this hard growing up. Elaine Gordon, in her extraordinary journey, never gives up hope. She reveals how she finds inner strength from her mother's love to become an "Unbroken Vessel."

- Nora Karam, Former Elementary Assistant Principal

One cannot wait to read with anticipation, the tenderhearted stories that lie within the pages of "Unbroken Vessel." Gordon displays true resilience and self-reliance as a young child with her unrelenting pursuit to overcome, arising from the unwavering love for her mother.

I had the pleasure of reading Elaine Gordon's memoir. It's an easy read and the pace is fast. Various chapters and events bring out the nostalgia of the past, the sense of security that community brings, and the need we all have to be loved and be safe. Life for Elaine was not always safe.

The book reveals a life that has had both challenges and triumphs. Certainly, life gave Elaine a rough start, but determination combined with love and support of one person—in this case her mother—has caused her to have a loving and kind outlook in life, instead of a sense of victimization and self-pity. Elaine Gordon is an incredible person today because of what life's lessons have taught her and it is my honor to call her my friend. A must read.

- Gloria Brown, MS, ORT, CHT

"Unbroken Vessel" Is raw and tender, full of life and disappointment, happiness and devastation—an affirming and full of hope story. In finding her authentic voice, Elaine Gordon has shown that adversity does not define who you are or who you will become ... the overcoming, that is the treasure! This is a life that exudes all emotions possible.

- Paula Rankin, Texas Educator – Certified – 4th Grade

The book echoes with experience, and Elaine Gordon does a wonderful job of telling her story in her own words in "Unbroken Vessel." Her writing style is unique, thorough, and entertaining. If for no other reason, this book should be read to restore one's sense of idealism and faith in moving forward to effect positive change in the world where love and forgiveness is concerned.

-Peter Gall, Professor of Mechanical and Aerospace Engineering, West Virginia University, Former NASA Langley Research Center, Aerospace Engineer

"Unbroken Vessel" is written by Elaine Gordon, a graduate of the Institute for Integrative Nutrition, where she completed our cutting-edge curriculum in nutrition and health coaching taught by the world's leading experts in health and wellness. We recommend you read this book and be in touch with Elaine Gordon to see how she can help you successfully achieve your goals.

- Institute for Integrative Nutrition

Unbroken Vessel

Elaine Gordon

ACKNOWLEDGEMENTS

Institute for Integrative Nutrition School (IIN) -
For many years, I have been encouraged to write my memoirs and finally I have made the commitment through my school's book writing program, "Launch Your Dream Book Course." In doing so, I have had many dear friends and family members motivate me to finally sit down and write my story. Not everyone is listed in my acknowledgments, and if you have played a part in inspiring me to finally share my life's journeys on paper, please know that I also hold you dear to my heart. Thank you all for helping me make my dream come true. These are just a few special mentions in the first of a series of several books that I am writing for my memoirs. As I continue to write the next several books of my life's journey, many more of your names will be included in my acknowledgements.

I'd like to express my gratitude to the following:

MARIE MILETI, my late mom, FRANK MILETI,
my bro and SHAVAWN GORDON-RISSMAN, my daughter...
I decided to dedicate my first book to all three of you because during the first twenty years of my life, I would not have survived without the love from all of you. Your stories are throughout my pages and darling daughter, your story will continue. Thank you for loving me as you have done. I have been molded by all of your love.

PAUL GORDON, my eldest son -
There are no words to express my love for you. Thank you for always being there for me, loving and encouraging me throughout my years of raising you. What a joy and honor it is to be your mom. You have brought me many honors and have become an incredible human being and father to my first granddaughter, Sawyer. I love you son for the goodness you have contributed to our world.

ENOCH, (JONATHAN DAVID GORDON) (AKA, AIRSHIP ENOCH), my youngest son -
Mothers of artists and musicians are very special and understanding people. My love for you, son, goes very deep. You have brought into my life so much color and love. Yes, I do know you are my son, as unique and different as you are, because I was awake when I gave birth to you. You are as beautiful to me as the beauty in a sunset that God paints most evenings. Although, you have changed your name and have become an incredible musical composer and producer, you will always be my amazing son, who I held in my arms when you were very young. I am privileged to have a son such as you.

NATHAN RISSMAN, my son-in-law -
"The perfect man," as you have been branded. I am so blessed to have you in my family. I am thankful for your love and concern, not only for me, but also for being a loving husband to my daughter,

Shavawn, and the most perfect father to my first grandson, Charlie. I love you greatly.

HEATHER GORDON, My stepdaughter, and
SEAN GORDON, my stepson -

You both have grown to become incredibly loving and responsible individuals—thank you for the love you have both put into your own sons. I am thankful that I have had a part in your lives, and although I am not your biological mother, I will always love you and consider you my children.

VINCENT CALDERONE, my engrafted father -

I realize that you are not my biological father, nor a blood relative; you have impacted my life more than you know. I am so grateful that I have been fortunate enough to have a second (or even a third) chance at having a father who loves me. I only hope that I can be a daughter who loves you as much as you have loved me. Thank you, too, for being as tough on me as you were. You benefited my life and your toughness was always seasoned with love.

HERBIE GRIPER -

My late common-law stepfather Although you were not with me past my pre-teens, I will never forget the wonderful things you taught me. I was also grateful for you being there during mom's hard times, so that I would not have to handle all the burdens alone. I miss you in my life, and I know you would be pleased to see how my life has developed. Thank you for filling in the gap for our family and my love, honor and devotion will always be there for you.

FRANK MILETI, *my late father* -
I know you have not been there for me throughout my life, however, I do want to say that later on in your life you took steps to show love and kindness to me and for that I am grateful. No, you have not been the father that I hoped you would be, but at least you left behind a loving stepmother for me, and a baby half-sister, who is a doctor today. I love and forgive you Dad—I realize that you are the man that God chose to be my father and you did your best to be a loving father in your 80's and 90's. And for that, I love you unconditionally—rest in peace, Dad.

SALLY MILETI, *my stepmother* -
You have been a wonderful stepmother to me and I have enjoyed learning all about the Chinese culture from you as you were born and raised in Malaysia. I appreciate the love and compassion that you have shown to me and how hard you've worked at helping my brother and me stay involved in the family. You truly are a gift and a beautiful gem in life, and I am thankful for you.

ELIZABETH MILETI, my youngest sister -
Although you are younger than my daughter and older than my sons, you have been a wonderful example of what one can do when the right love and support is in place. I am happy for you little sister, and I am very proud of all your accomplishments. Thank you for being the sister that I never had growing up.

ANGELIQUE BOWMAN, my half sister -
For many years I did not know you even existed, but through a series of events I have come to realize that you too are another offspring of my father's. I know we have not spent much time together, however, I want to take this opportunity and moment to honor you and acknowledge you in my first book. You are a good-hearted person and I am hoping to get to know you better in the coming years.

MARY WATERHOUSE - my best friend
and Life and Health Coach from IIN -
Mary Waterhouse, your name truly rings true for who you are. You do "water" all who come in your path. I want to thank you for being in my life for the past 30 years and for coaching me through many of the events coming into print in my 2nd, 3rd, and 4th book. You truly are a mentor and a sage. Your wisdom exceeds your years, and your unconditional love for all surpasses whom you are. I love you Mary Waterhouse, as if we were sisters from the same womb. I

am grateful to you for your steadfast love and unwavering patience with me throughout the years. Thank you.

KIM NORTH, my incredible Editor -
Thank you for taking the time out of your busy schedule to edit my first manuscript. You truly are a gift to me in my life and I know that my book is better because of the work that you put into editing "Unbroken Vessel." Also, thank you too for our friendship—it's priceless!

ERNIE SANCHEZ, the best Graphic Designer -
Thank you, Ernie, for helping me design the front and back covers and for the layout ideas throughout the pages of "Unbroken Vessel." You are a good friend, and I am fortunate to have your expertise knowledge in creating a beautiful presentation in the first series of my memoirs.

DAV ANMED, an amazing Photographer -
I have seen many great photographers, but you surpass them all. Your talent and eye for photos is a rare gift. Thank you for making me look like a cover girl! You are the best!

ESTELLA FLORES, one of my god friends -
Many people accuse us of being sisters—I should be so fortunate. You are better than a sister to me and I am happy to say that life is a better place since we met. Thank you for lovingly styling me and for ironing and choosing clothes for me so that I would have a great presentation for the front and back covers of my book.

ALL OF MY MANY FRIENDS AND FAMILY -
There are too many of you to name, and I don't think my readers would appreciate reading an additional book inside my memoir about all of you. I am more than blessed to have so many wonderful people in my life that I love and appreciate so much. Thank you all for how much you have added to the richness of my life.

MY GOD, WHO IS THE CENTER OF MY WORLD -
Last but definitely not least, I am grateful to you, God, for your unwavering love, forgiveness and protection that have been there my entire life. I have had many conversations with You since early childhood, and I continue to talk to you as my faith grows. I know that you will always be there for me. Thank you for being the love that fills my heart.

Elaine Gordon

FORWARD

Elaine Gordon has been a close friend and life-coaching client for over 30 years. She often talked about writing an autobiographical/memoir book series, which I encouraged as I felt I knew her life sequence so well—it was dynamic. I knew that her early years were a mixture of hardship, poverty, disappointment, love, miracles, tenacity, betrayal and courage beyond belief. However, until I read her manuscript, I had no idea just how intense her life had been during her early years. Reading about the revolving doors of challenges that she experienced has made me appreciate her determination to always find a positive path, her authentic compassion and her ability to inspire others even more.

"Unbroken Vessel" is a memoir of a very complex and determined little girl who learned early in life that bad things happen, and good things can come from them. The good is most often determined by our conscious choice to view each individual, including ourselves, as a unique human being deserving of being seen, heard and assisted, if possible, in meaningful ways.

We are living in a time of personal, environmental, economic, political and societal uncertainty. It is a time when learning how to support humanity in even the smallest ways has become more important than ever before.

"Unbroken Vessel" is an extraordinary account of how one person managed to achieve this in her daily life regardless of circumstances.

Gordon does not espouse perfection and readily admits her own weaknesses while revealing the areas of her life that she wants to improve upon.

"Unbroken Vessel" follows Gordon from childhood through her late teens. Her subsequent books will detail the next stages of her life, which are further examples of how our willingness to experience growth and self-transformation contributes to a life that is fulfilling and that makes a difference in the world.

- Mary Waterhouse, M.A., CHHC

Unbroken Vessel

Elaine Gordon

MY STORY

The memoirs of my life story have been equated to a water vessel that cannot be broken. "Unbroken Vessel" is the first of several books in a series on my life's experiences that I am continuing to write. My first book spans a period of twenty years, from my birth to my daughter's birth. The subsequent books will continue my journey through two failed marriages, domestic violence, homelessness and despair.

Travailing through ominous years of poverty, my brother and I grew up on welfare in the housing projects of New York City's Lower East Side. The projects were a rough place to live. I endured many years of violence, including being threatened with a knife, a gun and being physically and sexually abused.

My father only lived in our home until I was five years old and left without warning. My mother, who loved my brother and me, was a good woman and was devastated when my father moved out. My mother had severe health issues that prevented her from working and in turn became addicted to prescription. She also began to drink heavily after my father left.

Growing up in this kind of dysfunction was "normal" for me—I thought most families lived this way. Through it all, the greatest gift my mother imparted to me, in spite of her difficult life, was the gift of loving others. She had a wonderful heart, and she gave me the confidence to believe in myself and the courage to accomplish my dreams.

I became an adult at seven years old, taking care of my mother. I wrestled with the idea of being under my mother's authority because I had so much responsibility as a young child. My mom depended on me for strength and support to such a degree that childhood was not an option for me.

This type of maladjusted life only taught me that boundaries were not important. This led to a pattern of dysfunctional choices later on in life. I realized after many years of great anguish that I had to work on myself to become the person that I was meant to be.

I have lived on welfare, but I've never felt poor. I knew that you would not get to Park Avenue by only a bus ride, but by educating yourself, having a good work ethic and determination. I also realized that you could create your own future by visualizing and projecting the life you would like to obtain. Taking bold action and working towards your goals, having faith in God and yourself, can lead to many accomplishments. I realized that this is the formula I needed to move my life towards a life of success.

I am writing my story not to focus on the defective lifestyle that I grew up in, or even had as a young adult, but rather to leave you with a gift of hope that you too can change the outcome of your life. This can only be accomplished by changing your mindset about your life and not focusing on what you had to endure, instead choosing to make a difference by loving and caring for others and believing in yourself.

The pages of my book can be graphic at times and I apologize about being so transparent. However, I wanted you to experience the life that I endured and still walked away a better—not a bitter—person. You too may have terrible things happen to you, and it's up to you to turn those experiences around.

If we allow ourselves to get bitter, then we are no better than the people or misfortunes that caused us harm. I encourage you to read my story and understand that in life we have so much to be thankful and grateful for, even though at times it does not seem that way.

One of my favorite sayings that I live by is, "I am not defined by what happened to me, but rather I am defined by what I do with what happened to me." Thank you for sharing my life and journey with me. My desire is that through my experiences I will help you understand how to love and forgive others and yourself by becoming the person that you were meant to be.

- Elaine Gordon

Elaine Gordon

INTRODUCTION

Many people equate health in terms of the physical body. My journey deals with attaining not only the healthiness of my physical body but also the healthiness of my emotional, mental, spiritual and intellectual parts of my being. This is what's known as our "Primary Foods."

These are the foods that we feed our bodies with first. The way we accomplish this is by making sure that all of our relationships are in a good, healthy state.

Certainly, our bodies need the proper movement and exercise to prevent us from becoming sick. Movement of the body helps us build bone density and muscle mass that will support our skeletal frame to assist our bodies in thriving.

Another area of our primary foods is our spirituality. Embracing a spiritual side helps us go beyond ourselves and causes us to know that we are not alone and that there is a powerful God in our universe that will guide and protect us throughout our lives.

The other vital primary food is our vocation, "our career." Whatever we decide to do in life, we should focus on the purpose, "why are we doing what we are doing?" Go beyond the daily grime of our everyday work life and see how many wonderful things we can do to help others, which undoubtedly gives meaning to our lives.

Take a look at this part of your life as an opportunity to have a greater impact for loving, sharing and becoming an instrument that's utilized in encouraging others.

These are the areas that assist the sustainability of our health and emphatically bring us joy. The good foods we choose to ingest into our bodies also contribute to a superior quality of life.

I was not able to witness a healthy example growing up with a mother that was in poor health, however, I did learn from my mom that besides "health being your greatest wealth," she also preached, "Having my health, I had everything."

A woman, my mom, who never knew what a healthy lifestyle was about, was so insightful. I am so thankful to her for teaching me those very life-saving principles.

My goal in writing this book is to walk you through my perilous journey of sadness, loss, disappointment and abandonment.

However, I chose not to leave my story there. All of my trials led me to an overwhelming love, joy, peace, fulfillment, forgiveness and sense of triumph. I see the silver lining in everything that I have experienced. We can all attain love, joy and peace by having a thankful and grateful heart in all situations. Go beyond current realities by visualizing the beauty that is attainable.

My hope and prayer for you, my dear reader, through my humorous and heartbreaking stories, is for you to become a better person rather than choosing a life of bitterness. I want to encourage you and give you hope that there is a whole world out there for you. All you need to do is pursue persistence in achieving your dreams, despite any challenges you are faced with.

Thank you for allowing me the privilege of sharing my gift with you—my life experiences through the pages of my first book, "Unbroken Vessel," which definitely contains innumerable cracks.

Elaine Gordon

Part I

Born on an Island - Manhattan Island

Elaine Gordon

Chapter 1

An Early Christmas Present

Restlessly pacing around on the third floor of a rickety tenement flat on Sullivan Street in New York City's Lower West Side, my mother gathered the iron and ironing board to prepare for the evening. She tested her iron with a drop of saliva on her finger and began pressing her laundered maternity blouse, as she was preparing for an exciting event. Unexpectedly, she felt sharp pains erupting from her abdomen that were well calculated apart and causing her great anguish. Marie Red, as my naturally redheaded mom was nicknamed, murmured profanity under her breath towards her large protruding belly.

"Not today. You are not going to be born today," she proclaimed as she continued to iron in spite of her excruciating pain. She was determined to attend her best friend's "high society" wedding that she had waited six months for.

Upon arriving at the wedding chapel, her labor pains became increasingly stronger and were now every five minutes. Barely a word had been spoken before tsunami-force water gushed all over the dance floor. Apparently, I just couldn't wait to break out of my cramped cocoon and meet the world head on.

Immediately, mom was helped into her brother's car heading straight to St. Vincent's hospital in NYC's Village area. Uncle Benny, my mother's favorite out of seven brothers, followed one of NYC's finest, while a second police car trailed behind speeding through the streets of downtown Manhattan as if they were VIPs with an escort.

My mother was in agony as she felt the imminent pressure growing deeper in her body. Luckily, we arrived at the emergency room with time for the nurses to prep for delivery. I was quickly delivered, and at a mere five pounds, I barely escaped the incubator.

Mom's pregnancy had been difficult. My brother was born 11 months prior and she was crushed to hear she was pregnant again just three months after my brother was born. Now, I was born 10 days early—considerably before my scheduled due date on Christmas Day.

Mom became very ill after my birth with a form of blood poisoning and ended up having a hysterectomy due to complications from the birth. When I was unruly as a child—which was quite often—she'd remind me that I was responsible for "breaking her baby machine."

I was pretty happy to know that my brother, Frank—nicknamed Chickie—and I would be the only two kids in the household. Life seemed to be moving along fine as my parents and I lived with my grandmother in the district now known as SoHo. At the time, SoHo consisted of abandoned, empty warehouses built in the late 1800s and early 1920s. In the winter, the tenement apartments became cold and drafty, and at six-weeks-old, I developed bronchial pneumonia. My chances of survival were very slim. My mother smoked cigarettes during her pregnancy with me, and it not only caused a low birth weight, but also a compromised immune system.

Struggling to stay alive in a small, enclosed oxygen tank at 6-weeks-old, a Catholic priest administered the last rights in the Neonatal Intensive Care Unit at St. Vincent's hospital. Mom's tears covered the glass enclosure, as I fought for life. To the amazement of the doctors, medical staff and clergy, I miraculously pulled through. I had a strong spirit of survival. This was the beginning of an unswerving and invincible attitude that would blossom as I became older.

In the words of Winston Churchill, "Never, never, never give up." This became the motto I lived by. I realized I was born for a greater purpose, and this was just the starting point. My indomitable spirit would guide me to withstand numerous challenges and hardships as I traveled down the road of life.

Unbroken Vessel

Elaine Gordon

Baby's Survival

Shortly after I survived the Neonatal Intensive Care Unit, my mother became very ill. My brother and I were temporarily put into an orphanage since my father's employment took him away from us the majority of the time.

My father served many years in the Naval Forces as a frogman— now known as the Navy Seals— before being stationed across the East River at the Brooklyn Navy Yard in the reserves. My mother once told my brother when he asked how we were both born in the same year, "Well, your father only came home on the weekends!" To make ends meet, my father also took on the job of a private investigator.

My grandfather's sister, my great Aunt Terry, could not handle the fact that my brother and I were being cared for in an orphanage. Lovingly, she quit her job, brought us into her home, and cared for us for a year.

I had a wonderful relationship with both Aunt Terry and my grandfather, Sal. He was a quiet man and an artist who owned several antique stores in Brooklyn where he was a gifted restorer of valuable antique paintings.

Sal taught me how to draw. I was not born with the painting or sketching talent that he was; however, it was a creative way to spend time with him. His love for my brother and me was unconditional.

The day finally came to leave Aunt Terry's house and return home leaving Aunt Terry with a deep void in her life. Sadly, my mother had become a stranger to me. It took me several months to warm back up to her.

My mother was a feisty, first-generation Italian-American woman. My grandparents both migrated to the United States from Italy through Ellis Island in the early 1900s and settled in NYC's "Little Italy." After living at my grandmother's house, my father, mother, brother and I moved to the Lower East Side of Manhattan, which was the beginning of a very different world.

Our family moved to the housing projects, and for a short time was quite nice, even though they were designated as low-income dwellings. We had a spectacular view of the East River and the neighborhood was relatively safe and pleasant. The days my father lived home with us were such wonderful memories. My life was protected and safe until our Lillian Wald Housing Project quickly grew more dangerous.

Father contemplated purchasing a home in Hicksville, Long Island, where he felt would be a better place for our family to live. To the contrary, my mother did not want to leave the city, her family and friends, who resided across town in the West Village. Unfortunately, that did not benefit our family, as my parents grew apart from their disagreements and incompatibility. Dad was a loner and preferred to have a life of quiet and peace, while my mother was a social butterfly and a live wire.

Even as a young child, I felt the tension in our household. Although my mother was a good-hearted woman, she didn't always have patience and could be heavy-handed when it came to my discipline. An example was usually at meal times. I was not the easiest child to feed and would fuss quite a bit around dinnertime, preferring to play rather than eat my dinner. When I was almost three years old, my mother was attempting to feed me, and she completely lost control. In her frustration, she hit me on the back of my head causing the area above my lip to forcefully smash into the corner of the kitchen table. I had to get several stitches and don a sizeable bandage on my tiny face. My father was extremely angry with my mother and things seemed to go downhill from there.

Life moved on as my brother and I were approaching our fourth birthday. Even though we could feel the tension at home between my parents, I was very happy to have both of them at home with us.

Elaine Gordon

Jersey Shore Summers

Summertime was always exciting because we spent it in Asbury Park, on the Jersey Shore. My brother and I enjoyed long days of summer fun, swimming and playing with new friends.

My father—in typical fashion— was only there on the weekends. By this time, he was in the reserves and working as a private investigator for the Burns' Detective Agency. He would spend a lot of time with my brother and me. This was where he taught both of us how to ride a bicycle.

I was approaching my 5th birthday and I could not believe he was not holding onto the bicycle as I rode down the dirt road. That was the beginning of discovering what wheels were all about, and my love for cycling began.

My brother and I were inseparable and so many of our memories as siblings remain. At various times, I would forget a detail and he was always there to fill in the blanks for me. I don't know what I would have done without my brother. You would have never known that during our growing years together, we were complete opposites. He was an introvert, quiet, smart and very laid back. I, on the other hand, was compared to a heat-seeking missile, moving at lightning speed until I reached my target.

We loved each other and truly were best friends. We often played for hours together. One afternoon, we discovered a summer camp on the opposite side of the woods from the bungalow where we were staying. We decided to hike through the tough terrain, and peek through the fence.

This one particular day, a camp counselor happened to see us as we were crouched down and nestled deep inside the blackberry bushes. She called for us to come around through the large gate that was used for service vehicles. We headed in that direction, and to our surprise we somehow landed on their stage to be introduced to all of the other children who
were residing at the camp.

We were more than embarrassed. Ironically, the lesson the camp counselor was teaching that day was to reach out and make friends with others. How apropos it was for us to be there that day. We received a small award for being good sports and letting the camp use us as an example of what it meant to "make new friends."

Such a fun day it was. As we headed back to our bungalow through the woods, to our surprise, we encountered a man with a very large pitchfork. That was the day when I learned what a good athlete I was. In fear I ran what seemed to be a 5-minute mile. Chickie, on the other hand, walked.

After returning from our very exciting adventure, I saw the girls next door playing outside. They were coloring in a very large coloring book, and I asked if I could color with them. To my surprise, one of the girls, who had red hair and lots of freckles, drew a square on the side of the page. She told me that I had to color inside this small square, perfectly, before she would allow me to color in her coloring book. I colored very carefully, struggling to stay within the lines. Being inexperienced at coloring, my fine motor skills were definitely not developed enough to suit her liking. Consequently, I did not make the cut.

Soon, I heard the voice of my mother calling me after her return from the local market. She handed me a carbon cardboard drawing board, which was popular at that time. The neighbor girls quickly ran over to see what my mother had given me. Jumping up and down with excitement, they asked to try the new drawing board. I took the board's pencil and drew a very tiny square; so tiny you could barely position the point of a writing instrument inside the square. I looked up and said to the girls, "If you can color inside this square, you can try my carbon board." There is always something to say about karma.

Days at the bungalow were long and entertaining, and the weekends at the summer rental were filled with laughter coming from many of my aunts, uncles, grandmother, and my parents' friends who drove in from the city to enjoy the lazy summer days at the Shore.

I have such fond memories of my family being all together, enjoying each other's company and playing various card games that we all enjoyed. Life was good for a four-year-old who would be turning five, soon.

Unbroken Vessel

Elaine Gordon

Chapter 2

The Empire State Building Shoplifter

Splatting onto the concrete, you could hear a loud curdling scream as blood filled my mouth—I had lost my two front teeth at the age of four. After learning how to ride through the wooded area of our rented summer cottage in Asbury Park, I still managed to take a spill. My ability to bite into a juicy red apple was now sorely affected.

Once back home in the projects, I quietly encountered my father loading his gun for work, as he did every day, but this particular morning something very different occurred. My dad had decided to take me along to shadow him at work. It was "take your daughter to work" day and I was thrilled to tag along.

Elaine Gordon

At the time, the Empire State Building was the tallest structure in New York City—very impressive for one so young as it appeared larger than life looming over the city. My father's work assignment was to visit every concession stand on each of the building's 102 floors that were open to the public. Dad gathered his note pad and pen and proceeded to question each concession stand employee about any shoplifting that had occurred.

After what seemed like several hours to investigate these crimes, we finally arrived on the 102nd floor to go out onto the observation deck and take a look at the grand view of the New York City skyline. I anxiously anticipated gazing my eyes through the observation viewer at the edge of the deck when I was abruptly interrupted by my father's stern look and puzzling questions. He looked down at his tiny daughter's pockets, bulging and overflowing with various goods, and asked, "What is that in your pockets Elaine, and where did you get those items from?" In a sheepish voice I replied, "When we stopped at the stands, I was so happy that they were giving out candies and toys to take, just like on Halloween!"

I had helped myself to whatever I wanted. I thought how nice it was to have everything laid out on a shelf so that I could see what I truly liked, rather than pick from a tiny little bucket. By the time we got to the top floor, I had no more room in my coat pockets.

Not surprisingly, Dad was not amused. He swiftly gave me a swat on my bottom before proceeding back down to every floor to embarrassingly explain that during his own investigation, he had a very tiny shoplifter under his nose, helping herself to whatever she fancied.

As I wiped away my tears, I felt so disappointed about not getting to look through the giant scopes on the observation deck. Luckily, after hitting all the floors to the bottom, my father decided to take me back up to the observation deck and allow me to have a look through the magical looking glass. He had kept his promise to me about looking at the view, and gained an entertaining story to tell along the way. This was a memory my brother and mother would never forget.

Elaine Gordon

Dad's Desertion

Saturday morning bath time was always fun for me especially when I could play with my brother's toy soldiers, covered in bubbles. I was especially excited today because my mother was throwing my 5th birthday party that afternoon. My brother had reached the same age first and would turn six in 39 days. As I soaked in the bath, I thought about the beautiful red velvet dress my father had bought me that I could hardly wait to wear. Turning five-years-old, I felt so grown up.

Suddenly, shouts and screams interrupted my thoughts, "What was happening outside of my bathroom door?" I thought to myself. I heard my father shouting at my mother, and my mother was crying. I tried to listen and all I could hear was muffled noise until my mother's words rang out loud and clear. I heard mom's pleading, "Why are you leaving?" My father, who was very reserved and unemotional at times, told my mother that he was not happy being married and was moving out.

After hearing the front door slam shut, I quickly drained the water from the bathtub and got dressed. When I emerged, I saw my mother at the kitchen table, crying. I asked if she was all right. She wasn't able to speak. I hugged and kissed her and said, "Don't worry, mommy, everything is going to be okay. I am here to take care of you and help." Even at such a young age, I knew that I was more than a little girl. I always felt older than my years, even at five years old.

My mother managed to pull herself together because, in just a few hours, we were having a house full of people. Many of my aunts, uncles, and cousins would be arriving with my grandmother and my mother's best friend, Marie.

My grandmother was the most amazing woman—a tiny and old-looking Italian grandmother. She always wore a mid-calf black dress, black stockings, and a black turban on her head, following the death of my grandfather. Tessie, as she was called, suffered from rheumatoid arthritis, and smelled like Bengay topical ointment most of the time. She also wore garlic around her neck to keep away evil spirits. Grandma had sixteen children, however, only nine survived—my mother being the youngest.

She was very loving and would come over every week and bring fresh smoked Italian mozzarella and hot Italian sausage, which were my favorite. When she visited, she was always so kind to my brother and me. She would give us $5.00 each, which back then was the equivalent of around $50.00.

As the birthday festivities were getting ready to start, my mother, with deep sadness in her eyes, got all dressed up. I remember wishing I could do something to make her feel better. When I blew out the candles on my birthday cake, my wish was that my dad would never leave home.

As relatives and friends were starting to arrive, I quickly ran into the bathroom and hastily got dressed in my beautiful dress. This time I heard lots of noise and laughter outside the bathroom door and I thought to myself "today is my birthday party" and I was so excited that it was my special day.

I emerged to find all of my aunts, uncles, cousins, friends, and neighbors. I looked around the room and did not see my father anywhere. It made me feel quite sad until there was a sudden, loud knock at my front door. A very pretty, tall woman with light-colored hair, I did not recognize entered. Behind her was my father.

Surprised to see him, I started running up to him until I saw someone behind him—a little girl about the same age as me, wearing the same red velvet dress I had on. I didn't know who this little girl was, but this was my birthday party, and my father bought me the same dress to wear for my birthday. Why?

I quickly turned and ran into the bathroom, crying, not understanding why this girl who was at my birthday party, with my father and this strange woman, had the same dress. My father came and took me out of my bathroom and tried to stop me from crying. He brought me into the living room to introduce me to the little girl. Later on, I found out he had bought two of the same dresses—one for me, and one for his new girlfriend's daughter.

My 5th birthday will always haunt me … not only because my mother was so sad, but also because this was the last day my father would ever come home again.

Unbroken Vessel

Elaine Gordon

Conversations with God
(a parent in first-grade shoes)

Days were tough after my father left home. My mother suffered from so many health issues as she only had one working lung. Despite having emphysema, which worsened steadily, she smoked four packs of mentholated "Kool" cigarettes a day. She also drank heavily, compounding her health issues.

I would walk home alone from first grade most days of the week unless one of our neighbors would walk with me. The times when I would walk home alone, I would pray to God that my mother would not be drinking and I would get home safely.

I had these conversations with God most days of the week as I walked briskly toward the apartment. The projects were becoming scarier for everyone, especially a little girl. Walking through the local public swimming pool park located on Pitt Street, I'd see junkies and perverts in the stairwell outside of the park, shooting up heroin and exposing themselves.

As a young first grader, these types of violations began to rob me early on of my innocence. I would have to run home as fast as I could so that I would not find myself in a dangerous situation.

The projects where I lived had 14 stories with nine families on each floor. Our apartment windows faced the main entrance to the building. All who lived in the building would have to pass our kitchen and bedroom windows to enter. There was always a large amount of traffic coming and going through the building's entrance, and the people in my building truly felt like extended family, often greeting our little family as they passed by.

Most days, when I would finally make it home from school, my drinking suspicions would be correct. I would hear music playing in the living room, usually Dinah Washington's song, "What a Difference a Day Makes," or Johnny Mathis and Tony Bennett—her favorite records when she was drinking. I would find my mother sitting in the kitchen, and instantly cop a bad attitude and demand if she was drinking. I felt, in my young life, that I had become the parent in first-grade shoes.

When she denied drinking, I would persist, mentioning the music and the way her eyes looked. She would insist that she was not drinking alcohol in her coffee cup. I'd start opening up kitchen closets and drawers, yelling at her, "Where is your liquor?" My mother liked to drink Manhattans—whiskey, sweet vermouth, bitters, and a maraschino cherry. As my rage swelled, I'd eventually find her drink somewhere like behind the toaster.

One time I picked up her glass and smashed it in the kitchen sink and ran outside, slamming the door behind me. I didn't like to see my mother drinking and at times the only thing in the refrigerator would be a bottle of half-full wine.

Mom was a very loving woman when she was sober, and she actually taught me how to love and accept all types of people. I loved that about her. She also loved me with a passion; however, she hated my smarts, and the way I behaved when she was drinking. I just wanted her to be in control of her own life, rather than feeling like I had to bear the responsibility of taking care of her at such a young age.

I started feeling the responsibility a few days before my seventh birthday. My mother and I were outside of my building. The weather was icy-cold and she admitted feeling so secure with me.

I puffed out my chest and felt as though I was on top of the world. "A grown adult feels secure with me," I thought proudly.

I was only a child and was obviously not truly capable of taking care of an adult. For some reason, I always felt older in my body, which at times caused me to make poor decisions, without the proper guidance from a father and stable mother. I did not have much experience and knowledge about life, or how to take care of myself, let alone an adult parent.

But I am thankful that my mother taught me how to be a softer person on the inside, rather than the hard and callous person that I projected to the outside world. She spent a lot of time cultivating love in me, trying to soften the colder, indifferent side that I was developing. I also knew my mother truly loved and cared about what happened to me, and even though she had many problems and difficulties she faced every day, psychologically, she was always there for me.

I don't know how I would have turned out or survived in this world if she had not taken the time to help me find a balance between toughness and love. I attribute her great gifts of kindness, love, compassion, and empathy that she passed down to me, to be the main reasons why I feel love for people throughout the world.

If it had not been for her steadfast love and commitment towards me while growing up in one of the most dangerous welfare housing projects in New York City, I would not be the woman that I am today.

Elaine Gordon

Gangrene Venom

(house call gone bad)

Over the weekends, my mother use to hold card games in our apartment. Many of her friends from the building, and from my grandmother's Italian neighborhood, would come over and play all weekend. My mother would cook food for the players and also get paid a small percentage from each new card game that was played. This was the only way my mother was able to make some extra money since she was unable to work due to her illness.

I particularly enjoyed when the company would come over to our place because usually in the morning, I would find lots of quarters on the floor from the evening before. The result of someone being so excited that they won the card game that they would throw some quarters on the floor. They often remarked that it was for the cleaning lady—me. Yes, I would clean up after every card game. The good news, however, was that I got paid handsomely from the quarters that I found on the floor.

Elaine Gordon

My apartment window was on the ground floor directly over a small area of grass, bushes, and dirt. There is something about dirt and kids that are inseparable. I used to play outside in the dirt on a regular basis, and I was not the best at washing my hands afterward. One day, while I was playing in the dirt, I noticed that my fingertips were getting infected from playing in an area that more than likely was not very sanitary. As the days passed, one of my fingers got worse.

One particular weekend, when the neighbors and friends came over to play cards, I was not feeling well. I went to bed only to have my mother wake me up in the night to observe that I had a very high fever. Unfortunately, it happened to be New Year's Eve and many of the doctors who would visit your home when you were sick were not available.

My mother and one of my mother's friends, Vinny, who was there playing cards, drove me to Bellevue Hospital—one of the best hospitals in New York City. Because it was a holiday weekend, there was not a physician available and the hospital advised us that we should head back home and they would call a physician to come over to my house. We obliged and before long the phone rang, and a doctor from the hospital was on his way to my apartment. I was about eight years old, and my fever had spiked to 104 degrees.

When the doctor arrived, he noticed that my finger was infected. He felt that it would be necessary to cut open my finger, right there on our dining room table, because he said there would not be enough time to take me back to the hospital.

The card players quickly cleaned off the table and placed a clean white sheet on it to make a sterile environment. The doctor asked my mother to place me on the dining room table so that he could proceed to clean out the infection as gangrene was setting in. He was concerned whether or not I would lose one of my fingers if the gangrene progressed.

I was keenly aware that something was going to happen to me, and decided that I was not going to let this strange man put a horse needle into my finger. Vehemently, I protested, as I did with every needle that headed my way. Five of the male card players tried to hold me down so that the doctor could inject the anesthetic into my finger. I looked like a scared animal fighting to get away. I put up such a powerful fight that all of the five men couldn't even hold me down. After quite a lengthy struggle, the card players finally had me subdued while the doctor proceeded to inject my finger. I was so enraged, that I bent over and bit the doctor on his hand.

My limited experiences with doctors usually turned out disastrous. At one of my regular pediatrician check-ups, when I needed to get a vaccination shot, my doctor had to chase me outside of her office and onto the street. Lifting up my dress by the curb, she let me know who was the boss by administering the vaccination. Dr. Steinbeck was a tough German woman who did not take any sass from an eight-year-old.

My mother was beyond mortified as the doctor finished up a frenzied surgery on my dining room table. When the entire procedure was over, I had to remind her that she promised me a reward for going through this difficult medical procedure. Let's just say, if looks could kill, I would no longer be here.

There are times in our lives, whether we are young or old that some things are better left unsaid. As the days passed, my finger healed and life in the projects went back to normal.

Unbroken Vessel

Elaine Gordon

Confused Climate

As I got older, I realized that being a fast runner was the by-product of living in such a dangerous setting. It was difficult being one of the only girls in a building filled with aggressive boys. Growing up with people shooting up heroin in the stairwells of my building, I had to learn how to run up 14 flights of stairs, two steps at a time, to visit a friend on the 14th floor, or to look at the view of the East River from the rooftop. I had to be alert, sharp and fast.

There were times when I would be outside of my building sitting, on the curb when some of the neighborhood boys would attack me and touch my body until I would get away from them. It was a game to them until I managed to run faster than them and could desperately run into my apartment and lock the door.

My mother would question me, and I could not verbalize what had happened to me until later in the day. My mother would bravely go outside and stand up for me. It was such a good feeling to have my mom take care of me when I really needed her to.

The one thing that I missed learning was setting up proper boundaries in my life, as far as drawing the line when I had been violated either physically, emotionally, spiritually and even sexually. One such incident I can vividly remember when I was in second grade. After a long hard day at school, I was walking home having my usual conversations with God about my mother, when I arrived home and found her very angry. I was not sure what had happened, or why she was so upset, but I knew she had been drinking for several hours.

Looking back, I understand why I was so often angry with her. It was times like these I wanted my mom to have milk and cookies for me after school, instead of hiding her drink in some obscure place with that give-away music playing in the background.

This particular day was no different than most, except instead of interrupting her and running out of the house and slamming the door, I decided to challenge her and go head-to-head with her. I directly confronted her about her drinking, truly hoping to come to some resolution. I didn't realize at eight years old I could not fix her problems. As we got into a heated argument, my mother, out of frustration, grabbed my arms to restrain me and did not realize that her long fingernails were digging into both my arms.

The next morning as I was preparing to go to school, I walked into the kitchen where she was sitting, and she took one look at me and the imprint of all ten fingernails evenly distributed on each arm. She started to cry. I hugged and kissed her and told her that it would be all right because I could wear long-sleeved shirts to school instead of my usual short-sleeved blouses that typically accompanied our Catholic school uniform.

When my mom was not drinking, she was my best friend, as well as my mother. The best memories I have of my mother are when she was sober and how much she helped me with my schoolwork, especially my spelling assignments. Thanks to her, my brother and I were the top spellers in our school and it was usually the two of us battling it out during spelling bees.

I loved her very much and she gave me so much confidence. It was hard for me to let down my guard but she usually saw right through me. The thought of my past behavior when I was angry and disrespectful as a child saddens me. However, that was the only way I could have survived in such a rough neighborhood with a home life continually on shaky ground.

Although we did not eat healthy all the time, mom also made the best breakfasts in the world, and her cooking was truly amazing. One of my favorite snacks was Rice Krispy Treats. Now, as a board-certified Integrative Nutrition Health Coach, I understand childhood food cravings and the comfort eating that goes along with it.

I also realize that the body is an amazing repair machine. I probably should be dead with all the junk food I ate as a child, however, I've learned it is never too late to change your eating habits. I am grateful that my life involves helping others to get healthy, both physically and emotionally.

Our emotional health is also tied to our primary foods—the "first foods" we feed our body. My area of expertise as a Holistic Health and Nutritional Coach is specifically the primary "food" of relationships, not just what we ingest into our bodies. Relationships of any type can cause the body to become sick if they are dysfunctional. That is why relationships are called the "first (primary) foods" we feed ourselves to maintain our health. I have often thought that in the area of relationships I have failed horribly, so I decided to take on the challenge of studying and applying the knowledge of what a healthy relationship really is.

One of the other wonderful things my mother taught me was the power of positive thinking. She was my biggest cheerleader, even though we had many rough patches. I feel that I have learned to love and forgive, look for the best in people, and not take things personally. She truly was a lovely, gentle, kind and giving soul underneath her addictions, and I loved her greatly. I started learning how to compartmentalize the pain and suffering and began focusing on handling the household as adults would do. I realize now that my formative years also set the stage for a tolerance for violence without any boundaries, yet despite that I also learned to cultivate a loving heart and a forgiving spirit, making me the person I am today.

Elaine Gordon

Chapter 3

The Housing Project Lifestyle

Growing up in a housing project was a different lifestyle than most would imagine. You learn the art of dancing and fighting in this street culture. Every Saturday morning the neighborhood kids would gather in the main lobby hallway and play, dance and flip-gamble baseball cards.

I was very good at flipping baseball cards, which helped me win more valuable cards. You had to flip at least five or more cards so that they would land on the ground either all facing up or all facing down. At times you could have a mix of both, and the next person had to match each card on their next turn. If they did not match your cards exactly, you won their cards. I had a knack for this sort of thing, and I usually returned to my apartment with most of the neighborhood kids' baseball cards.

There were always kids playing outside in front of our building. One of the games we played was "Johnny on the Pony," where the kids would line up against the brick wall of our building and bend over modeling a row of horses. The other team, with the same amount of kids, would run and jump on their backs as if they were riding a horse to see if they could hold them up as they recited "Johnny on the pony" three times.

We tried rocking back and forth on their backs with the hope that the team under us would collapse. The key to this game was gaining the advantage by having the biggest and heaviest person on your team to outweigh the opposing team and cause them to fall.

The games we played as children in the projects were different than most games played by children in the suburbs. My friends were usually much older than my brother and I and the games were quite rough. Another game I enjoyed was a game called "Hide the Belt." One of the neighborhood kids would borrow his father's big black Garrison belt—a big, thick leather belt with a very large silver buckle. Then one of the kids would hide the belt in the bushes, as the rest of us would stand on the outside stairs, which was home base.

With our backs turned and our eyes closed, we waited until the person who was hiding the belt let us know that it was time to find it. The person who found the belt would chase all the other kids, whipping them if they caught them. Only the fast runners could make it back to base without getting whipped. This game was violent, however, the reason I liked it so much was because I was one of the fastest runners on the block. I knew how to dodge and weave like an NBA basketball player, and no one was able to catch me.

Usually, when it came time to play tag or some other sort of running game, I was the first person to be recruited on the captain's team. On the other hand, my brother had a problem with sports. He was the slowest runner in the neighborhood, and the team captains usually argued who would have him on their team because he was always their last pick and he usually got eliminated first. If he was in a ball game, and they saw me coming to the park, poor Chickie was thrown out of the game to be replaced by me. I felt so sad for my brother as he usually went home, crying.

When the city had their annual sports competitions at the FDR Drive Park, many of the inner-city kids came out to compete. This was our version of the local Olympic-like games where you had a chance to win notoriety along with the gold medals from the city. My brother and I were always in the same races and I always made it to the finish line first, in record speed. One year I took home ten medals to my brother's none. My brother always wondered why he came in last—in everything!

My brother and I were in the same class for eight years of grade school at Our Lady of Sorrows Catholic School on Pitt Street. We were both "A" students and made the honor roll every year. I used to wonder how my brother always scored higher than I did on our grades when I never saw him study, and I studied diligently every evening.

When we were adults, he confessed that he had stolen my homework almost every night and copied my answers. I found this simultaneously disturbing and yet quite amusing. If I had known that my brother had cheated on his homework when I was younger, I would not have been so amused.

We wore uniforms to school every day and I was glad about that because growing up on welfare, we did not have a lot of disposable income for clothing. The money that my father actually sent for a short period of time was never enough to support a family of three.

Even living on welfare though, I never felt poor. I would take the metro bus uptown, by myself, to spend time at the Plaza Hotel. I would admire the beauty of the lobby and how ornate it was designed. I would walk into the café at the age of eight and order a cup of tea in a china cup. I felt as elegant as a princess, even in my torn and tattered clothes. I knew that you did not get to live and enjoy the beauty of Park Avenue, or even uptown's Central Park, by only taking a bus ride. It was by hard work, determination and a persistent attitude that would afford you the opportunity to enjoy a lifestyle in such a beautiful area.

I had always been a hard and smart worker ever since I was a young girl. At nine years old, I started working with several families ironing their shirts for a nickel apiece. I also spent my time selling my old comic books to bring in some extra money. At 10-years-old I babysat. Project living certainly caused me to grow up very early in life. Along with the dysfunction that I had at home—mom's alcohol problem and addiction to prescription medications—I took on being responsible for my mother and brother. A task that was overwhelming for an adult, let alone for a young child in grade school.

My mother's doctor would come over to our apartment when she was not feeling well, and inject her with morphine. She would always ask me to sit with her in her bedroom afterward because she was afraid of how the drug made her feel. I always did my best to help my mother feel at ease.

I don't remember being a child where life seemed innocent and protected. I grew up with a sense of obligation to take care of my small family. I always felt in charge of my household. Even though my brother was slightly older than I was, he was much more apprehensive and careful than I was.

My strong personality caused me to inherit a level of responsibility that was not appropriate for a person so young. I was left no other option because I was the only one who dealt with all matters head-on. I struggled with two worlds, whether I was an adult or whether I was just a kid who did not know any better.

Unbroken Vessel

Elaine Gordon

Night Terrors

Forceful shaking awakened me out of a deep sleep, as I tried to make sense out of my mother's frantic pleas for help. In a panic, she told me that she was dying because she drank too much alcohol and took a considerable amount of sleeping pills.

I was eight years old, and I had to think quickly on my feet not knowing what to do. I told my mother to sit down as I jumped out of bed and ran outside into the hallway of my building. I started screaming and knocking on as many doors as I could to get some help. Some of the neighbors came over and one, in particular, spent the next several hours walking my mother around the house to keep her awake.

Growing up in this kind of atmosphere was more than sobering. I learned how to compartmentalize very early on; otherwise, I don't think I would have mentally survived.

Regardless of living in such a dysfunctional environment, there were also many good memories of my growing up years. The very best days were those days when my mother would cook for the neighbors. She was so happy to serve and love others through her cooking. She would tell me to eat healthy because, as she liked to say, "If you have your health, you have everything." I only wished she had heeded her own advice because smoking and drinking like she did, really took a toll on her life. She did not live past the age of 42 years old.

I still miss my mother to this day, and even though her life was brief, I remember so many wonderful things that she taught me. Most of all, I remember how tenderly she'd hold me and tell me how much she loved me. This was the greatest gift my mom bestowed on me. Her love enabled me to have the will, strength and determination to keep moving forward, and look beyond my circumstances. I can now envision a life where I can truly make a difference in the world.

I truly believe that love has endless power—as the power of love can heal any broken heart.

Unbroken Vessel

Elaine Gordon

Pint-Size Punk

When I was young, you would find me playing outside and not interested in learning how to cook or do the things that most little girls loved to do. I became a tomboy, as tough, athletic girls were called back then. I preferred to play baseball, stickball and run around getting dirty like most of the neighbor boys. I disliked playing with paper-doll cutouts, having tea parties and playing with dolls. I was much more interested in climbing trees and experiencing the athletic and adventurous side of life.

I loved baseball and was so disappointed when the city baseball league would not allow girls to play in Little League. I would watch heartbroken as my brother played, and I was forced to be a spectator.

I played handball across the street in the park regularly, and at 10-years-old took the bus and the subway to midtown Manhattan to play on a bowling league. I felt so grown up being able to travel by myself to do the things that I loved. One Saturday morning, my friend's father saw me waiting at the bus stop and asked me what I was doing there all by myself. I proudly told him that I played on a bowling league and was on my way to the bowling alley. I remember how happy I was to tell him about my journey. My friend's dad looked perplexed as he was much more protective of his daughter and would never allow her to travel by herself.

It made me realize, had my father stayed at home with me growing up, I would not have had such unaccountable freedom. I would have had a much tighter rein on my choices and surely a more balanced life. I am convinced that the number of mistakes I made would have been drastically reduced.

But I was a student of the "school of hard knocks"—not necessarily the best way to learn about life. I wished I had had the guidance, love, and teaching from both a mother and father. I believe if I had a more stable base in my life I would have made better choices, and eliminated a lot of pitfalls growing up.

Elaine Gordon

First Holy Communion

Project living wasn't really the place to wear too many nice things, especially not beautiful lacy dresses with ribbons and bows adorning the sleeves, collars, and hemline. I preferred to wear dungarees, or shorts and a T-shirt. The summer weather in New York City was humid and blistering hot.

On one particular weekend, I was making my First Holy Communion and I had to wear a beautiful lacy dress with ribbons, bows and pearl embellishments. Perched on the top of my head was an exquisitely beaded mesh veil that was terribly burdensome for a girl who loved to don a baseball cap.

The ceremony was divine as I angelically walked down the aisle on the red carpet, hands folded and head bowed to receive the sacrament of the Holy Eucharist—the receiving of Jesus Christ. As a child, I did not fully understand this concept, however, I knew in my heart that I loved God and felt very close to Him. After all, I did have conversations with God most afternoons as I walked home alone from grade school.

After the ceremony, we got a car ride in my Uncle Benny's car. We were happy we didn't have to walk and enjoyed the ride home through the mean streets. Once home, I could not wait to get outside and play ball. As Mom and the relatives prepared a banquet for the festivities, my mother peered out the window and could hardly believe her eyes. There I was all dressed up with a baseball glove in my hand, my bouquet in the dirt, playing catch. She had hoped that for just this one day, I'd behave gracefully, instead of wanting to play baseball in an elegant, white communion dress. It took a lot of coaxing to yank the baseball glove off my hand and get me to come inside to join the party. It was quite a memorable day of laughter, joy, and an enormous amount of Italian food.

After eating all the delicious food that I could, I needed to go outside again and see who was around to play. I saw many of my classmates parading around with their bouquets in their pristine communion dresses. While still wearing my white dress, I decided to head over to the playground and slide down the sliding pond and play on the seesaw. I loved the seesaw. My neighborhood definitely had a bit of an edge to it—sometimes kids would slide off their side when you were up in the air and cause you to come crashing down hoping that your foot wouldn't get caught under it.

This actually happened to me that afternoon while I was playing on the seesaw with my friend. I nearly broke my foot but thanks to quick reflexes, the top of my foot only got bruised. To add injury to insult, I decided to walk to the side of my building where I saw a wooden plank over the grass and dirt tempting me to make it from one side of the wide board to the other side, without falling. No chance—the plank suddenly shifted. I swiftly launched into the dirt wearing my dazzling, white Communion dress, now transformed into a soiled, ripped ensemble. My mother was furious because I had to wear that dress to school the next day for a church procession. She spent several hours washing and sewing it for the following morning and did not mutter a word to me all evening.

I should have listened to her advice when she told me not to get any stains or dirt on my dress. It would have been more prudent if I had changed my clothes before I went outside to play. But again, that usually was not my style.

Elaine Gordon

Chapter 4

Grandma's House

Saturday morning was always the best day of the week for me. I would spend the weekends at my grandmother's apartment in the West Village. The neighborhood was predominately Italian with laundry hanging outside on clotheslines from the windows of many of the apartments. The smells of Italian sauce and Italian dishes permeated the downtown streets.

Like many other immigrants who migrated from Italy through Ellis Island during the late nineteenth century, my grandparents settled in this area of New York City. America was seen as the land of opportunity and New York City became the gateway to freedom for many families.

Elaine Gordon

My grandmother, Tess, spoke fluent Italian. My favorite uncle, Benjamin (Benny) Bufano, also lived with my grandmother. He was named after my great uncle, Beniamino Bufano, a well-known famous sculptor. You can find many of his works of sculptured granite throughout the streets of San Francisco and in nationwide museums.

When I visited my granny's house on the weekends, she would often times give me a tiny glass of beer in the morning, along with my cereal, while I watched Saturday morning cartoons. I often wondered if she gave me the brew because of my elevated energy levels in the hopes that it would calm me down.

We would spend the entire day at the market and the cheese store, Joe's Dairy, where they would make the best Mozzarella in the city. Recently, the Italian cheese store closed its doors after nearly 50 years of devoted service to its loyal customers. It was located across the street from Saint Anthony's church where my parents got married, and my brother and I were baptized. St. Anthony of Padua Church, the official name, was established in 1859 and was the first parish in the U.S. that specifically served the Italian immigrant community.

We would also visit a tiny grocery store called Willie Kepp's, where the aroma of freshly-baked bread spread throughout the streets. The owner, Willie Kepp, particularly took a liking to me. Upon arriving at his store, he would greet me with a big smile and hand me a sweet treat. He often remarked how much I resembled my mother, except for her red hair, when she was a child and visited his store.

I really enjoyed spending time with my grandmother. Often, we went for long walks up the block that would take us hours. She would stop and chat in Italian with many of her neighborhood friends who were also immigrants from Italy. While I waited for my grandmother, in between nudging and pleading with her to move on, I would amuse myself by swinging around a light post. We eventually would make it to Bleecker Street, close to a mile away, and continue to shop at the local meat store until our grocery bags were full.

On alternate Saturdays, we would stop at one of my other uncle's houses on Broom Street. Uncle Brownie as he was nicknamed, had a chicken slaughterhouse. It was the only house in the neighborhood that doubled as a business. Grandma would pick out live chickens and Uncle Brownie would slaughterer them—oftentimes in front of me. Visiting my Uncle Brownie was not my favorite place to go.

On occasion, when we headed back to my grandmother's building at 117 Sullivan Street, my Uncle Benny would be waiting for me in front of the building. He would take me over to the Malt shop a few doors away and buy me a drink called an "Egg Cream," or a small bottle of espresso coffee soda called a "Manhattan Special."

I loved spending time at my grandmother's house because it was one of the few times in my childhood, I felt like a kid. To top off my day, before it was time to head home, my Uncle Benny would take me over to the local toy store and buy me something of my choosing. Saturday mornings felt like Christmas. Granny and I would head back towards the Lillian Wald housing project on a bus that traveled east on Houston Street. It passed the infamous Bowery where many homeless people lived. We would finally get off the bus on Avenue A and proceed to walk about five long blocks to my building at 484 E. Houston Street, close to FDR Drive.

It always felt good to be back home with many of my friends hanging out in front of the building, getting ready to head to the park across the street to play several games of handball.

Unbroken Vessel

Elaine Gordon

West Side Story

Life for me was like living on both sides of "West Side Story." On the one side, living on the weekends at grandmother's place where I learned how to be a little girl who enjoyed shopping and cooking; where it just felt so good to be taken care of. On the other side of the fence, coming home to the projects meant picking up where I left off, being responsible and in control of my family.

Living in the projects also taught me how to fight and dance. The projects were an interesting mix of people. We had predominantly African Americans and Puerto Ricans in my building, and most of the surrounding buildings were a block away in "Alphabet City"— avenues A, B, C and D. Just a handful of Caucasian, Italian, Jewish and Irish people lived in the building next to us.

My building was comprised of mostly males. They were the worst troublemakers, but the best dancers around. One of the things I loved as a young girl was to dance. I would spend hours in the hallway learning to dance from the neighbors and perfect my moves. I also spent a lot of time fighting.

Yes, I was a scrappy nine-year-old that walked around with a tough attitude and a hood walk, or a "bop," as it was called. I felt like I was the toughest kid on the block. Many of the older neighborhood boys would keep an eye—they figured that I only had BB's in my pocket, instead of cannons. The older boys, who often compared me to a peanut, were always concerned that something would happen to me as a result of my tough attitude. I guess guardian angels do come in all shapes and sizes.

One day there was a man in my house and my mother introduced him to me as my Uncle Tommy. Uncle Tommy was not my uncle, nor a blood relative. His real name was Herbie and he came to live with us. He was a very good person and cared deeply for our family. What I did not know at the time was that Herbie and my mother met years earlier when they were pen pals together during World War II. Herbie was in the Army with my mother's three brothers, Chuck, Anthony, and Benny. They were all in a division of the U.S. Third Army that sneaked across the Rhine River at Oppenheim.

After the war was over, Herbie came home to the West Village to meet my mother. They fell in love and wanted to get married.

However, Herbie's grandmother was a very religious Orthodox Jew, who forbade him to wed a Gentile. Mom's Catholic Italian family also opposed the union.

In respect for Herbie's grandmother, who raised him along with his twin brother, he decided not to go against her wishes, or be estranged from his family. My mother's heart was broken as well as Herbie's.

Eventually, she met my father in a restaurant where she worked as a waitress. He ordered a Swiss cheese sandwich every single day. They got married and moved into my grandmother's apartment. Herbie, having a difficult time seeing my mother married, eventually met another woman and got married as well. He settled in Brooklyn, New York's Coney Island area, close to his family.

After my father left us, Herbie also went through a divorce and later reunited with my mom. They loved each other, and it was nice to have a home life that was happily balanced again. I was relieved not to have the sole responsibility of caring for my mom. Thankfully, Herbie was there to take over the reins for me.

I spent a lot of time with Herbie, working the cash register at his luncheonette in Midtown Manhattan. We also spent many hours at

Coney Island, making sand castles in the sand and walking over to his brother's house a few blocks away.

Life at that time was exciting. Herbie smoked cigars and drank beer with many of the neighborhood men in our building. The group of boisterous men would watch and yell excitedly at the Yankees playing baseball. I especially enjoyed when Herbie would on occasion take me to Yankee Stadium to watch the home team beat the other MLB teams.

Herbie made a good living working in the garment district in Manhattan. Unfortunately though, his gambling habit nearly ruined his life after he lost his luncheonette to his bookmakers.

In spite of Herbie's gambling habit, he was the best substitute for a father. Life was definitely easier for me, allowing me more time to focus on being a kid and struggling through the normal challenges of childhood like school, and friendships. Although Herbie was there to balance the scales, my mother continued to drink and Herbie handled the damage control with short-tempered frustration, and love.

Every building in our neighborhood had its own territory and the kids who lived in each building were protective of their closed group and contemptuous of others. There were times where I had a hard time making friends, especially girlfriends who lived in the building next to me.

It took me six months to make friends with many of the Irish kids who lived in the next building. I had to go through a tough initiation process where the kids were mean to me. Finally, after being persistent and resilient, I made my way into their circle.

It definitely helped that Herbie bought me a cute toy poodle we named Monty and a radio-record player. It was battery-operated and was able to play music outdoors, a precursor to the boom box. The difference was that you could play vinyl records, along with tunes on the radio. I was the only one on the block that could bring music outdoors, or to the park across the street. I became the most popular girl in the neighborhood.

Life was wonderful for me then. I picked up a few more babysitting jobs and continued to iron shirts for our neighbor, Louise, who was very particular about her shirts being ironed correctly. Louise was a close friend of my mother's. I remember the days when I would come home from school and my mother and Louise would be playing Scrabble. Mom was very good. I often played the game with her and developed a love for words.

I spent some weekends with my best friends playing games over at their building, and even attending the St. Patrick's Day Parade on Fifth Avenue. Even though I was full-blooded Italian-American, I loved to wear all green to the parade. From bows in my hair that adorned my long pigtails, to my T-shirt, pants, socks, and shoes— everything was green. It was quite a task to paint my penny loafer's green, but I wanted to show my new friends that I was truly in the spirit of St. Patrick's Day.

Besides, I was definitely outnumbered and was hoping to make as many friendships with my new Irish companions, as opposed to getting into fights with them, which seemed to be a weekly occurrence. My mother would know that I had been in another fight because I would crash into the door of my apartment, breathlessly locking the door behind me. She always eyed me sternly, staring at my ripped shirts, nose bleeds, and scrapes and bruises on my arms and legs. She barely said a word most times, but her piercing glare was enough to constrain me, until my next scuffle.

Yes, project living was a tough environment to survive in, yet this lifestyle taught me how to become resilient, discerning and very quick on my feet. If I had only had a running coach in my life, who could have trained me in track and field, maybe I would have had the opportunity to win the Olympics with gold medals hanging around my neck.

This was the beginning of my interest in becoming an athlete. Later on in life, I did fulfill that dream. I won several medals as a triathlete, and a competitive Black Belt Martial Artist, both nationally and internationally.

Elaine Gordon

Christmas Invasion

Christmas time was always the best time of the year for me. Being on the ground floor of our apartment was wonderful because we were able to see everyone who entered the building. I especially enjoyed decorating our windows facing the entryway with various Christmas lights, snowflake spray and colored stencils of holiday images. The residents who lived in the apartments appreciated our cheery holiday spirit, as Christmas music resonated from our place.

Aromas of my mother's gourmet cooking would pass through the window of our kitchen and many of the neighbors would follow the scent into our home. They would be welcomed with a warm glass of eggnog adorned with nutmeg and cinnamon.

Herbie, my brother and I would head up to Avenue D, which was only one long block away, to purchase a beautiful, large evergreen tree. The weather was always cold and snowy, and by the time we got home our noses would be red, and our hands and feet nearly frostbitten. We had such a great time decorating the tree, having hot apple cider and playing all of our favorite Christmas music. I cannot remember a time in my home that I was happier.

My brother and I would walk up to Orchard Street, which was quite a distance away, to buy Christmas gifts for our mother, Herbie and each other. We both had a limited budget, however, the prices were inexpensive enough to have enough money to buy everyone gifts.

We celebrated Christmas Eve after Midnight Mass at Our Lady of Sorrows church. My brother and I could not sleep that night knowing that Santa was going to make a stop at our apartment after midnight. We often wondered how he would be able to get into our apartment because we did not have a chimney and we had bars all over our windows. We wondered if Santa would land on the roof of our 14-story building and take the elevator down. After our discussion of trying to figure out how he would deliver our gifts, we would fall fast asleep.

Mother liked to wake us between one and two o'clock in the morning on Christmas. Even though it was officially Christmas Day, it still felt like Christmas Eve to me. We would hear laughter and commotion coming from our living room—usually, Herbie was there, along with our aunts, uncles, grandma and close neighbors.

We were always hoping to catch a glimpse of Santa red-handed. We would ask mom if she had seen Santa and she would say, "You just missed him playing cards with us. He was running behind schedule, so he decided to stay for a while and have some coffee and pastries." My family loved to play cards, especially on holidays, well into the wee hours of the morning.

I was always disappointed about not meeting Santa, but my mother explained that we were his first stop and he had to deliver all the other presents to the rest of the kids in our building. Chickie once said to me, "Next Christmas, we'll stay up all night, and catch him." One year my favorite gift was a basketball. I was the neighborhood's challenger, and sports were my first love. I also received a fantastic Navy pea coat, which was the fad this particular year. Along with my coat, I received a pair of tan desert boots, which were not only comfortable but also popular. What a monumental and memorable Christmas this was.

A few days later, the reality of living in the projects set in, as I wore my new coat and shoes to the local grocery store to buy my mother some milk. As I walked through the back park, which was a shortcut to the grocery store, a gang of teenage girls approached me. I was uncomfortable knowing that they were not just looking for directions. As they approached, I heard them laughing and murmuring how much they loved my new coat and boots.

I walked briskly trying to escape their comments until suddenly they surrounded me shouting that they liked my coat and shoes so much that they wanted me to give them up. There was no way I would hand over my favorite coat and shoes to this group of taunting girls, so I began to run towards the grocery store. The group of about eight teenagers caught me. I argued telling that they would not steal my coat, my shoes, or anything else I had.

Before I knew, they started attacking me and threw me to the ground. As I was on the ground getting kicked and punched, I held onto my coat and shoes like a lion holds a fresh kill. One of the neighborhood dads walked by as I was being attacked, curled in the fetal position, praying I would survive this mugging. The good man yelled at them to leave me alone, and they all ran away. He then gently helped me up, brushing me off and remarking how strong I was without giving up my belongings. He cautioned me, that in the future, I needed to be more careful because this gang of girls could physically harm me with knives or guns. He advised me if it happened again, to give them what they wanted because my life was definitely worth more than the material possessions I had. I am not sure I agreed with him at the time, but he was wise to caution me.

Afterward, he walked me to my apartment and explained to my mother what had happened. Mom thanked him and turned her loving attention towards me and attended to my wounds. I started to feel better especially when she gave me some milk and chocolate chip cookies, which are my favorite. I was grateful that I still had my pea coat and desert boots to enjoy.

The next morning I was outside playing when I saw the same gang of girls who attacked me. This time I saw one of my friends, Peaches, whom I had met a few months before, with the group. She often referred to me as her "little white buddy." I had no idea that apparently Peaches was the ringleader of this band of girls. After she discovered what her group of girls had done to me when she wasn't there, she started slapping the girls. She shouted at all of them, that if they ever hurt me again, she would beat them unmercifully.

I don't agree with fighting violence with more violence, however, I did feel justified in her response to her gang of girls. I also knew that living in the projects was a fight or flight survival mentality. I did learn from lessons like these that paying attention and being alert were the key to staying safe. I was thankful for good friends who protected me, and I was glad for neighbors who watched out for my well-being.

Elaine Gordon

Laguna Beach's Charm

One particular summer at home was especially difficult with my mother's continued drinking on top of her serious illness. She made frequent visits to the hospital due to coughing up blood. Her emphysema was progressing, causing her to have a hard time walking or climbing stairs. She would have to stop at least five or six times to catch her breath as she took her steps.

Her doctor was also making trips to our home to administer morphine for her chronic pain. She had a hard time sleeping as well, so the doctor prescribed very potent sleeping pills and tranquilizers. I was distraught to see her in such poor health. Herbie did his best to take care of her, but the doctors wanted her to be admitted to the hospital for further testing. At this point, I was extremely angry and unfairly blamed Herbie. In my mind, he was not my biological father and I thought if my real father were at home, my mother would be healthier and my life would go back to normal. In the mind of a ten-year-old, my critical reasoning skills obviously were not developed enough to come to rational adult conclusions.

I thought it was time to write a letter to my father who lived in Laguna Beach, California. I asked him if my brother and I could come live with him because mom was very ill. I had overheard the doctors speaking of the inevitability that my mom would not live very long.

I wanted to be with my father—my knight in shining armor—who would rescue my brother and me from a harsh life in the projects. I was not sure dad would receive my letter, but I found his address tucked away in one of my mother's drawers and took a chance.

To my surprise, my father wrote my mother a reply, and although I got in trouble with her for writing the letter, my dad's words assured her that we could fly out to be with him in California. He mentioned that he would take care of us while she got the proper medical treatments that she needed to get well. That meant leaving mom with Herbie to care for her, while we went to live in Laguna Beach.

My brother and I were very excited. We could not believe we would be moving to California and taking an airplane for the first time. My Aunt Jo flew with us to attend her son's wedding. The airplane ride was surreal. I fell in love with flying and jets that day. At the age of ten, I could remember the airline stewardess—as they were called back then—giving me my first pair of wings to pin on my blouse. I was so elated to receive my wings, and on that day, I decided I would pursue becoming a flight attendant.

Our flight seemed to take an eternity, but when I saw my dad at the airport all of my fears and insecurities vanished. My brother was exhilarated to see his dad and I felt on top of the world. We dropped my Aunt off at our cousin's house and spent some time visiting with the family, and then rode home to see our new house, and the rooms we were going to sleep in.

It was a beautiful quaint wooden structure that was up on a hill overlooking the Pacific Ocean and Catalina Island. I had never seen such beauty, and at times you could see dolphins and whales accompanying each other as they swam by. The back of the house faced the Pacific Coast Highway, and if it were not for the traffic going by, our home would have been the perfect paradise.

Life was wonderful living with my father. He quickly registered my brother and me at the local Catholic School, across the street. It was a great school and academically it was much more advanced than the school we attended in New York City.

My brother and I did well in school, and we met quite a few of my father's friends and enjoyed weekends at Newport Beach's Water Park. Life in Laguna was stable for me. I enjoyed the infamous Laguna Beach "town greeter." He was a man who stood on the corner welcoming everyone into Laguna Beach either walking or driving by. He was incredibly interesting, and I remember asking my father if I could take a photo of him. I also loved the Pacific Ocean sunsets and believed that God painted a spectacular sunset for me every evening.

After a few months of school and getting myself acclimated to life in sunny California, news came over the loudspeaker in our classroom that President John F. Kennedy had just been shot and killed on Nov. 22, 1963. I remember what a sad day that was for our nation, and all Americans. School was dismissed and my father, brother, and I had a conversation about what happened. My father was very intellectual. With all the years he spent in the Navy, he knew a considerable amount of information about our nation, and also intelligence from around the world concerning governments and politics.

My dad was also a world-class swimmer and had a flair for adventure. We got along very well, although he had a difficult time controlling me because my mom had given me so much freedom when I lived in the projects.

One day, as my father, brother, and I were clothes shopping, I drifted over to a clothing rack that hung the fashions of the day. I wanted a black skirt with a white blouse that seemed to be the popular choice for many of the girls in my class. My father decided that he was not going to purchase the skirt and blouse that I wanted but instead insisted on buying a dress for me embellished with yellow bows, lace, and ribbons. Being an aspiring athlete, the yellow dress did not appeal to my style and I would have felt more comfortable in the black pleated skirt and white blouse with a Peter Pan collar. For some reason, my father wanted to dress me as a little girl. I realize that ten years old is not very grown up, but given the responsibility I was handed by my mother, I felt strongly about choosing my own clothes.

I put up quite a contentious debate with my father, and when we returned home he not only spanked me with his belt, but he also threw me around the room. I reached out for a little cloth doll that my mom made for me and sent from her hospital bed. I suddenly missed her and felt afraid of my father. I could not wait until I saw my mother again.

Mom started getting well and wanted my brother and me to return home after we spent nearly half a school semester in California. Dad didn't want to send us back to New York City, so he asked my mother to leave Herbie and come to California to live. I was elated at the possibility of having my mother and father together again, and life looked promising for our family.

That weekend we were invited to our cousin Vincent's wedding. It was wonderful. The dancing, music, food, and treats were incredible. I also got to meet some relatives for the first time. Excited and thinking about seeing my mother in just a few short days, I went looking for my father during the reception. As I turned the corner of the reception hall, I saw my father holding a woman and kissing her. I could not believe my eyes. I ran into the other room and quickly found the door to the outside of the building. My father came running after me and said that he would explain when we got home.

Upon arriving home, my father did not explain who the woman was. He basically talked about the relationship between him and my mother. He proceeded to tell both my brother and me that he was not planning to get back together with my mother after all. He just wanted to have us in his life and he couldn't think of any other way that would be best for all of us, except having my mother live in California. I protested and cried and begged him to reconsider, but he was not speaking another word about the matter. I was heartbroken.

Meanwhile, back at our apartment in New York, my mother was under the impression that she and my dad were going to get back together. She was preparing to give up her apartment and move to Laguna Beach. This was terribly hard on Herbie as he loved my mother and didn't want to see her leave. He understood the reasons why my mother wanted to put her marriage back together, even though his heart was breaking. Herbie truly loved my mother along with Chickie and me. His love ran so deep, that he was prepared to let my mom move three-thousand miles away, for the greater good of our family.

Upon arriving in California, my mother was quickly acquainted with my cousin Vincent's new bride, Marlene—a beautiful woman who had a most caring and loving attitude. She became a good friend to my parents. One night, Vinny, Marlene, and another lady friend named Leigh went out to dinner with my parents. The waiters greeted my father and Leigh who obviously frequented the establishment often. Marlene and Vinny quickly interrupted the waiter to introduce my mother as Frank's wife. The waiter apologized for not knowing this and everyone continued to order their meal.

As time went on, this sort of thing continued to happen when the group would go out. My mother finally asked Marlene what was going on, and she explained that Leigh was my father's girlfriend. My mother was devastated. She spoke to my father and decided to move back to New York City where family and friends were and planned to take my brother and me with her.

My father asked if at least my brother could stay with him. Mom hesitated and asked my brother what he wanted to do. At the time, Chickie wanted to be with his father. He held back his feelings and never discussed with my father how much he would miss us. As our plane took off, my brother had a hard time holding back his tears as we headed home to New York City.

To our joy, Herbie held onto our apartment and refurbished the place with beautiful furniture. He was truly a great man, and I realized then how much he really loved all of us. He truly was the best father I could have ever had.

As the end of the school year approached, my brother decided he wanted to move back to the projects to live with my mother, Herbie and me.

Unbroken Vessel

Elaine Gordon

Black Sunday

Black Sunday is what I refer to when I think about the second day of January. This year it was not a very Happy New Year for me. This was one of the most devastating days since the day my father left home.

Herbie was preparing to head to Brooklyn to attend his niece's wedding while my mother was begging him not to attend. He was not feeling well that day and my mother wanted him to rest after the stressful holiday season. Herbie insisted that he needed to make an appearance at the wedding, and that he would be home early. He assured my mother that he would be all right and proceeded on with his plans to take the local metro bus and subway train to Brooklyn's Coney Island.

Several hours later, in Herbie's absence, my mother started drinking excessively. I didn't want to deal with her at that point, so I headed to bed earlier than usual that evening and hoped and prayed that Herbie would be home soon.

After saying my prayers, and falling asleep, I heard screams and crying coming from our dining room area, which connected to our living room. I quickly jumped out of bed with my brother trailing behind me, only to find my mother drunk, sobbing and screaming, "Herbie is dead! Herbie is dead!"

My brother and I could not believe our ears. As Chickie went over to console mom, I dropped to my knees and pleaded with God, "Please don't let this be true!" In the middle of my own tears, I crawled over to my mom and asked her what happened, and how did she know. She said someone who was at the wedding telephoned her that Herbie was taken to the hospital in Brooklyn, and they believed he had had a fatal stroke. He was only 44 years old and was relatively healthy. I don't remember ever seeing Herbie sick. His energy level was high, and he never complained about any ailments.

Mom's tears and her inability to stand up truly frightened me. I went to the phone and called a few neighbors who lived upstairs. It was now 2:00 in the morning. Neighbors quickly came to our apartment without a minute to waste. Glancing at the dining room table, where my mother had been sitting before the news, I noticed a letter she had written to him. She was mad at him for going and had written a very harsh letter, chastising him for not being home on time. Without my mother or any of the neighbors noticing, I grabbed the letter and decided to discard it, alleviating my mother of any extra pain and guilt.

As the neighbors were helping my mother and taking charge, my brother and I were in complete bewilderment and engulfed with intense sadness. This was our first experience of losing someone who was close to us.

My brother and I clutched each other as we both broke down and cried. This was a dreadful crisis in my childhood. Words could not describe the feelings that I was experiencing. Panic, fright, and abandonment consumed my thoughts. "What was I going to do?" "How would I take care of my family?" Thoughts of survival, responsibilities, and support became my immediate needs.

After an exhausting evening, I fell asleep on the couch wishing I were in some kind of horrible nightmare. When morning shined its bright light through the windows waking me, I realized that my fearful nightmare had become a stark reality. Herbie, my dad, was dead.

The funeral arrangements lasted several days, and my mother and brother went to the Jewish temple where the memorial services were being held. Because my mother was not married to Herbie, she had to sit in the back of the temple. I remained at a relative's home because attending the funeral was too painful for me.

One of the hardest things that my mother had to endure was watching the honor and condolences go to Herbie's ex-wife and daughter, who sat in the front of the synagogue. My mother felt as though her position as Herbie's soul mate and partner did not count, plummeting her back into a deep depression. I began to pick up the pieces, and resume my role as mother's caretaker once again, as I was barely about to turn 13 years old.

Unbroken Vessel

Elaine Gordon

Chapter 5

Life Not So Usual

Life had been much more stressful after the death of Herbie. With all my schoolwork, and helping more at home, my body was becoming weak. For weeks, I hadn't felt well. Acting like a grown-up was wearing me out. I was not equipped with the proper abstract reasoning necessary to handle so many burdensome situations. I was confused by the role I was expected to play at home.

One evening, the teenagers in my building were planning a big party on the tenth floor. I really wanted to go. Taking it upon myself to attend the party, Mom and I had one of the worst arguments I can remember. Her intuition was signaled; she put her foot down and would not let me attend. She was rightfully concerned about my safety with the older teenagers.

In hindsight, I'm glad my mother won this argument because this type of party was way beyond my comprehension of consequential danger. I had already been robbed of much of my childhood innocence, and I'm thankful my mother stuck to her parental authority this time and won the battle.

After getting back into the normal routine of life, I noticed that mom would still be sleeping when I got home from school at three o'clock. I would wake her with a kiss and ask if she needed anything. She'd drag herself out of bed and prepare some after-school snacks for me. I found escape watching my favored TV shows "Superman," "The Three Stooges," and "The Mickey Mouse Club." They lightened the mood from the actual life I was living. Many afternoons, I would try to cheer my mother up by sharing tales of my school day.

Neighbors were very good to us and mom eventually started cooking again and made her favorite gourmet meals for our neighbors in the building. We always had young people hanging out in our apartment, as mom was also a great source of wisdom and compassion for many of them.

A few months later, my brother and I were preparing to make our Catholic confirmation at our church. As I was attending the ceremony and preparing to receive the sacrament of confirmation,

I started feeling very weak and sick again and had a hard time maintaining myself in church.

Afterward, my mother had a small family gathering at our home that included some of the neighbors. She noticed that I was not my usual, energetic self, and discovered I was running a high fever. She rushed me into a cab and headed to the emergency room at the New York Infirmary hospital. I was familiar with this hospital as my mother was a frequent patient. This time, it was my turn to be admitted. I was terrified to sleep in the hospital, away from my mother and brother, and I especially hated when the nurses took blood out of my arm every day.

I was diagnosed with mononucleosis, which was referred to as "the kissing disease." I assure you, I was not kissing any boys, but was hospitalized and isolated for two weeks because the disease was highly contagious.

I was completely run-down, with an immune system that was highly compromised. My mother and grandmother had to wear masks, hospital gowns and gloves when visiting me. My brother was too young to visit, and I'd wave to him from the window, as he waited outside.

Being a grade schooler, two weeks seemed like an eternity away from home, especially in a hospital bed. I'd busy my days making clay model busts of famous people. One of my favorite sculptured pieces was of a pirate's head. I was so proud of my work the day I finished and couldn't wait to show my mom. Before I had the chance, a young boy from the hospital room next door came running into my room. He saw my clay masterpiece, ran straight towards my artwork, and destroyed it. I started crying and screaming at him. Nurses ran into my room to see what the commotion was about. The young fellow got reprimanded, but not severely. Upon my mother's arrival, I relayed the whole incident with tears. She comforted me and brought my favorite dessert—a jelly donut. I created my very own specialty by cutting the jelly donut in half and adding one scoop of vanilla ice in the center. This made me feel better, after the trauma of my destroyed creation.

Times like these strengthened the bond between my mother and me, and our love for each grew exponentially. I considered her my best friend and someone who knew me better than I knew myself. She would often refer to me as someone who had "a hard exterior but was a soft marshmallow on the inside."

As I grew in years, the difficulties that I endured had softened me, as opposed to developing me into a bitter individual. I reflected on becoming a better person rather than becoming hateful. Difficult things happen to all of us in life, especially during childhood. I found that if we look for the positive side of things, in the midst of suffering, that is where thoughts transcend into the beauty of life. This is how I found happiness within myself.

I started focusing on others and what I could do to help them, rather than dwell on how badly my life was, and the pain I carried. Despite her faults, my mother cultivated in me a lovely outlook on life—molding me into the compassionate, tender, loving person that I am today.

Elaine Gordon

Neighboring Girlfriends

500 E. Houston Street was the building next door. I had a lot of girlfriends there, in contrast to my building where I was the only girl who hung out with the guys. It was refreshing to hang out with girlfriends because I learned how to dress up, especially on Easter Sunday, and enjoy what many 13-year-old girls do. Lazy afternoons on Saturday were spent at my friend Michelle's house, where we played with cutout dolls—a novel concept for me.

Still maintaining my athleticism, however, I was one of the top handball players in town. Many of my newly found friends would walk across the street to the big park and play handball on most days. If you played a good handball match and won, you would move on to play the next contender. Being very good at the game, I played for hours. By the time I got home, my hand was swollen from playing. I was not able to afford a handball glove to offset the pain that goes along with playing the sport. It didn't matter how swollen my hand had become, because I loved the game so much.

Besides playing handball, many of the kids in the neighborhood would swim at the local public pool. The summers in New York City are humid and blisteringly hot, so swimming several times a week would be a fun way to cool off. At times, we would even open the fire hydrant and cool off in the heavy spray of the water. This always prompted a visit by the local police who would shut off the fire hydrant and reprimand us before escorting us to our apartments. That never went over well at my house and I was usually sent to my room.

Snowy, winter days were always fun in the projects because we hauled our sleds outside and slid on the man-made hills in the backyard grass. I used to dare myself to go down the hill, and successfully glide under the enclosing chain link fence bordering the grass, that was fairly low to the ground. By lying face down, with your body flat on your sled, you were guaranteed—sometimes— that you wouldn't crash into the bottom of the fence.

There were times when I didn't clear the fence and I returned home with red marks and bruises all over my neck. My mother was very well acquainted with my mishaps. She would grab ice from the freezer to help with the swelling and then fix me a meal and serve my favorite dessert, "Rice Krispy Treats."

It was days like that when I loved being a kid and coming home and just hanging out. Mom was happy, and that made me smile. What a lovely woman she truly was.

Another activity I enjoyed was ice-skating at Central Park and Rockefeller Center. My mother thought that I might want to pursue an ice skating career, however, sports such as these were costly. I managed to continue my passion on the ice though using the money I made ironing shirts, cleaning houses and babysitting. It was at this time that my love for business and entrepreneurship started to take root and would continue to grow throughout the years that followed.

Elaine Gordon

Adolescent Turning Point

The pre-teen/teenage years are a time of drastic change, especially for girls. My body started changing, although many of my girlfriends developed before I did. I usually avoided facing my back to them because I didn't want them to see that I was not a "turtle" yet, which meant you wore a training bra and you were fair game for someone to come up behind you and snap the elastic band in the middle of your back. Some pressures at age 13 were simultaneously humorous and stressful. Eventually, I made the "turtle" club and life moved along.

Eighth grade was the end of my grade school years. It was a busy time for me applying to Catholic high schools throughout New York. My first choice was St. Alphonsus High School in SoHo, my grandmother's neighborhood. Because I spent many weekends there as a child I felt at home in this neighborhood as I have always considered SoHo my second home.

My high school was considered a commercial high school where you mainly studied business and secretarial courses. The school was only a three-year high school, which would allow me to graduate at the age of sixteen. One of my close friends, Karen, who was in my class and lived by me, also got accepted into St. Alphonsus High School.

Although the school was only across town, there was not a bus that ran along Houston Street for us to take. I had to take a metro bus, then the subway to get to school. One day, traveling to school, the train was extremely crowded. I was in my Catholic school uniform—white knee socks and penny loafers—when a very well dressed man in a suit proceeded to exit the train. I was standing holding onto the rail as he passed me. He reached down and grabbed me around my bottom, nearly pulling me outside of the train. I felt frightened, embarrassed and violated. The ride took quite some time to reach my stop, and then my shaken-self had a difficult time walking the rest of the way to school. I cried all the way there as I made it to the entrance of the building. I wiped away my tears and headed to my class. I would never forget what that violation felt like. I never discussed it with my mother, but rather buried this deep inside of me hoping the pain would eventually be forgotten. After that day, I would take a taxi to school at least once a week—as the ride was only 15 minutes across town—as opposed to an hour by taking the bus and subway train. The taxi gave me some sort of comfort at least one day a week. I would use my babysitting money to take a taxicab when it was extremely cold. This was much better than bracing the elements when it was zero degrees outside.

My high school years were also exciting. The school was an all-girls school. Many of my classmates and I would lean out of the windows and yell to the boys who were waiting outside on the sidewalk. Several times, many of us got in trouble with the nuns and were put on probation. It was worth it to see all those handsome boys outside, even though we got disciplined for breaking the rules.

Many of the girls who attended my school were from my grandmother's adjacent Italian neighborhood. The girls lived on Mott and Mulberry Streets, and many of my classmates had families that were affiliated with the Mafia.

I was once again glad that I had to wear a uniform every day since my meager clothing budget would barely buy me a new dress, let alone a new dress for every day. You could tell my Italian classmates had resources due to the fur coats and diamonds they wore to school on cold days. I was glad that you were only allowed to wear your normal clothes to school for a few days a year.

School was very stimulating, as I was a natural at business and office procedures. I made friends easily and did very well in school academically. I also tried my hand at acting, dodge ball and table tennis although my school was not equipped, as many of the other New York City high schools were, for athletics. Although I was still only 4'11" tall, I still hoped that I would make the five-foot club soon. Many of the boys in my building referred to me as "mighty midget." I was strong, built athletically and sported muscles that I hadn't earned—there is something to say about good genetics.

My running ability was developing such that I could run at lightening-speed. I still often wonder what would have become of my athleticism had my running been incorporated with a coach who could have taken it further. However, living on welfare, and having my refrigerator only filled with one bottle of wine, and barely enough food to eat, I quickly realized that I would never have enough money for running coaches like the public schools had. I knew that training to be an elite athlete in track and field was beyond my means.

My three years at St. Alphonsus were very memorable. I attended Friday night dances and basketball games at the Catholic all-boys school, taught by Franciscan brothers. Power Memorial High School was our "brother school." The basketball games were exciting as

I caught a glimpse of "Lou Alcindor," aka Kareem Abdul-Jabbar. He was tall even in high school, at least 6'8." I remember hearing that the school had to accommodate his large size by making him a special desk.

I enjoyed spending time at my classmate Grace Ann's Italian Mafia home. I could somewhat relate to her lifestyle, as my Uncle Wo Wo, was also a key player in the mob. We would spend vacation at Uncle Wo Wo's home during the summer and I would play with my two cousins, Vinny and William, in their large five-story home in Dumont, New Jersey. My uncle preferred my brother to me, as I would ask way too many questions, and answering my inquisitive kid questions was not done in the Mafia world.

Uncle Wo Wo, had a girlfriend and was usually not home the majority of the time. In return, Aunt Grace, my mother's only sister, was not happy and spent most of her days drinking. Uncle Wo Wo had a cold exterior and a scary poker face. One evening, as my mother, brother, and I, spent the Fourth of July holiday weekend at their home, my aunt and uncle had a very big argument. My bedroom was next to theirs and I could hear my uncle screaming at her to stick her head in the oven and kill herself. My mother was sleeping downstairs and she also heard the disturbing argument.

As dawn broke, the sun was brilliantly shining through my bedroom window and the warm temperatures enticed me to wake my cousins and brother up for a backyard swim. My mother did not go to wake my aunt after deciding to let her sleep a bit longer due to her exhausting argument the evening before.

As we were swimming outside and playing, my cousin's Collie got overexcited and bit me in the eye. After being rushed to the emergency room by a neighbor, I wondered why my mother did not join us on the ride to the hospital.

When I was returned home to my aunt's house, sporting a large bandage on my eye, I could sense there was a somber feeling in the air. I made my way up to the main living room and saw both cousins, my mother and brother crying. My uncle was sitting in the living room as well but had no emotional response. I asked them what happened and the news was absolutely horrifying to me.

My aunt, in her distraught state of mind, managed to go into my mother's handbag the night before and remove my mother's sleeping pills to ingest the entire bottle in an attempt to take her life. I felt despondent and was completely consumed with thoughts of my aunt and how this would affect the rest of our family.

Apparently while as I was in the hospital having my eye attended to, my aunt was in the same hospital having her stomach pumped. The doctors worked very hard to revive her with no success. The medication had already absorbed into her bloodstream, which resulted in her death.

My mother was very close to her sister. When my Aunt Grace would visit our humble apartment in the projects, she would often remark to my mother how much happier she seemed in her tiny apartment on welfare, than she was in her affluent home in New Jersey.

My mother never forgave herself for letting my aunt sleep as long as she did and blamed herself for her sister's death. I did not even know how to continue caring for my mother after that day. It was hard enough to help her after Herbie died, but with the absence of her only sister, and blaming herself, life was quite a challenge over the days that followed.

I have always been grateful for the strength that God gave me as a young girl. I knew He would always help me get through all of my difficulties, and He always has.

Elaine Gordon

Government Aid

Once a month, each family who was on public assistance would go to a facility to pick up the basic staples: powdered milk, peanut butter, cheese and rice and beans, courtesy of the Department of Agriculture. I felt uncomfortable going to the center so my mother would ask my brother or our upstairs neighbor, Sheldon—who was roughly a few years older than I was—to pick up the food. Sheldon was African-American and was a kind and jovial person. I remember his infectious laugh and his willingness to help my mother with whatever she needed. He was a good family friend, and I appreciated him.

I spent a lot of time with Sheldon traveling on the subway to Coney Island and enjoying the lazy days of summer at the beach. I would laugh so hard when he would tell me he had a sunburn. I would always ask, "Where is your sunburn?" as I did not realize with skin so dark that you could ever get burned. I had a lot to learn about people, and the diversity I was exposed to in my life taught me many valuable lessons.

Sheldon would also accompany me to my Italian neighborhood across town for the yearly Italian feast. The neighborhood would set up booths on the street and sell delicious Italian cuisine. I was always a bit concerned when Sheldon would come with me to the neighborhood because many of the Italians I grew up with, as a child, were extremely prejudiced. I was very protective of him, and even though the feast was a big public event, I would always walk briskly and encourage him to keep a fast pace as we enjoyed the festivities.

I had once witnessed an African-American male and a Caucasian woman walking through the streets of the neighborhood and was horrified to witness the Italian boys being violent to the black man for accompanying a white woman. The neighborhood boys used metal garbage can lids to beat up the black man. I screamed and cried for them to stop, but my little voice fell on contentious, depraved ears. I headed home sobbing and talked to my mother about the injustice I witnessed.

One of the loveliest gifts in life that I was privileged to receive living in the projects was a love for all people. My mother actually helped cultivate in me the character of treating all people equally. She loved everyone and her love was evident by how she treated everyone who entered our home. I am grateful to her for teaching me how to accept and love all people. People's color, race, creed, ethnicity or economic and social status has never mattered to me. What has always mattered most to me was their heart. I have always seen all people as equals.

Growing up on both sides of the infamous depiction of "West Side Story," I felt privileged to be raised in a non-racist background. I would often tell my friends who were African American, "Don't let my Caucasian skin color fool you, because I might look white on the outside, but I am a black person on the inside." I would continue my soapbox with declarations like, "Stick out your tongue, is it the same color as mine?" "If you cut your finger, is our blood not the same color?" My friends would look at me as if I needed glasses and we would all have a good laugh. That is what truly loving your neighbor is all about.

As summer was coming to an end and my freshman year of High School was behind me, I managed to pick up a few more inches, adding to my stature. Feeling elated at 5'2", I was convinced that the kids on my block would finally drop my nickname, "Mighty Midget." This was a dream I long awaited. When I finally finished growing, I stood tall at 5'4."

Elaine Gordon

Chapter 6

High School Life in SoHo

High school years were filled with anticipation and excitement for the future. I enjoyed attending school and excelled in my studies. We had an extra-curricular class in drama where I became the drama coach for a one-man play and worked with my classmate, Elizabeth, for a semester teaching her how to act and present her performance.

The night before the play was to open, my classmate had a bad attitude toward my acting teacher, Sister Mary Ambrose, which resulted in Elizabeth being dismissed from her performance duties. The drama instructor looked at me, and said, "Mileti, memorize this skit."

My birth name was Elaine Mileti, and at no other time did I dislike my last name more than at that moment. My drama teacher commanded me to take over the lead role and gave me less than 24 hours to prepare.

Shocked and terribly unhappy with her decision, I looked at her speechless. My heart started pounding in my chest, my palms became sweaty and my breathing became shallow. I cried all the way home from school on the bus and subway. When I arrived home, my mother was not sure what had happened to me. Explaining everything, my mom put her arms around me and told me that I could do this. Having a difficult time composing myself, I dried my eyes, headed for the bath, and grabbed my voice recorder. I soaked for hours in the bubble bath trying to absorb the entire dialogue.

The next morning, still gripped with fear, I headed to school and continued to practice my lines. While glancing at my cue cards, I entertained the thought of going AWOL. Although the thought was enticing, my conscience got the better side of me, and I decided to continue onto school.

When I arrived at school, I walked into my acting class, as if I was walking in slow motion.

Once the class was briefed on our presentations, we headed to the auditorium and prepared ourselves for the performance. In my particular skit, I had to play three different people and change my voice to match the different characters. Being overcome with fear of performing in front of a crowd, one of my classmates gave me an over-the-counter tablet called "Compose," to take away the jitters before the performance. It did not help. It altered my voice and raised it several octaves higher. It was difficult to play the older, gruff characters, and at the same time turn around and play a woman who was calm and composed. I am not sure how I pulled this performance off, but the crowd went wild and loved it.

That was one of the last times I volunteered to coach classmates, and after that, I was reluctant to place myself in any position that ultimately put the responsibility on me.

Elaine Gordon

Breaking the Rules

Many of my girlfriends back in the projects were attending Catholic high schools across the city, and this was a time in our lives when we were venturing out of our neighborhood, into a world that differed from our familiar lives.

My 15th birthday was significant because it was the year that I threw my first party where alcohol was served. In retrospect, I should have thought this through. Being underage, it was good to know that my friends lived next door, and no driving would be involved. This does not make a wrong decision right, however. It was a consequential effect of growing up in the hood and having your childhood robbed. As teenagers, we were already carrying the burdens that many of the adults in our neighborhood carried. My friends often spent the night at my house because I had more freedom than most. We were able to go out and come home late into the evening, long after curfew.

One time my friend Franny's father was waiting outside the next building over from mine, for his daughter to return back to my house. He had been calling my mother, who was sound asleep and never heard the phone ring. He was clearly concerned. Upon arriving at my building, we saw her father outside, frantically pacing up and down the street hoping to get a glimpse of the taxi bringing us back to my apartment.

We were petrified to get out of the cab in front of my building, so we had the driver drop us off in the back alley where we would not be seen. We were anticipating how to climb through the rear hallway window, which was close to six feet high. As we stood in the grassy area below the window, we plotted how to lift each other up so we could get in through the tiny space. We successfully helped each other climb into the window and quickly headed for my apartment. The phone was ringing, and I answered it. Franny's mother screeched on the other end, demanding her daughter return home immediately.

Most friends in the projects did not have fathers living at home, and I was happy for Franny, even though she got in trouble that evening for coming home late, that she had a father who cared about her and was in the trenches with her during her formative years.

That was one of the things I wished I had had. I had so much freedom and authority that I couldn't comprehend adult-mandated restraints about staying out too late. Some accountability and discipline, like being grounded, might have helped me escape a lot of the pitfalls that I had gotten into. On a positive note, I was responsible when my friends and I went out to the Italian neighborhood across town to hang out at the nightclubs. I always made it my responsibility to monitor my friend's drinking and make sure that they all got home safely.

I protected my friends who were raised a bit sheltered. They were not accustomed to as much freedom as I seemed to have inherited. It was a bittersweet approach to growing up, but I had learned street smarts and paid attention to my intuition and common sense. I highly relied on what kept me safe and trouble-free.

I spent a lot of time during my high school years hanging out in the Italian neighborhood's West Side with my three girlfriends, Michelle, Franny, and Karen. My mother's brother, Chuck, had just gone through a divorce and rented a very cool apartment in the neighborhood, where my girlfriends and I would hang out on the weekends. You could say that he was going through a mid-life crisis. He bought a toupee and started dressing like a thirty-something-year-old. He always enjoyed my girlfriends and me hanging out at his modern-style apartment.

One of my girlfriends looked as though she was twenty years old. She was tall and beautiful, and my uncle actually started taking a liking to her. She was underage, and he was about twenty-five years older than she was. She was only 16 when they started dating. My mother was very upset about this and had a talk with me about it. I lost respect for my uncle and felt that he used me to get close to my friends. The thought infuriated me, and I did not want to spend very much time at his house anymore.

The clubs in that Italian neighborhood were separated by the types of young people that frequented them. There was one club called the "Dudley Club," where many of the drug users hung out. Another one was the "Chateau Club," which consisted of a number of younger kids who had family in the Mafia. They dressed like young gangsters with diamond pinky rings, Italian knit shirts and sharkskin pants. My cousin Vinny was a member of this club.

The young guys were about a year younger than I was, and they spent a lot of time drinking and learning how to run numbers for the bookmakers. Many of them began their life of crime robbing semi-truck trailers and selling the shipments in the neighborhood as swag—stolen merchandise. One time my mother bought a color TV from them when color first became accessible in the marketplace. It turned out to be a rip-off, as it was an actual black and white T.V.

with a plastic color screen on the front. I mentioned to my mother that crime does not pay and buying stolen merchandise does not make for a good investment.

Many of the kids in my grandmother's neighborhood aspired to become Mafia recruits. A few boys, who attended Saint Anthony's grade school, would go over to the local park where some of the homeless people from the Bowery would hang out, and they would harass and torment them. The Bowery on Houston Street was home to many of the homeless, drug addicts and alcoholics on the Lower East Side. They would wipe your car windshield down at stoplights with dirty rags to get change for cheap wine. Usually, a wave of the hand would halt their attempts.

One particular day, while I was riding in a car with one of my friends, a man came staggering up to the car, high on heroin and started cleaning the window. To my surprise, this particular man happened to be my older cousin, Ralphie. I was stunned and did not know what to do. The traffic light turned green and we headed home. I didn't tell my friend who the homeless drug addict was. I didn't even have the words to describe what had just happened.

My cousin Ralphie was one of my Aunt Grace's three older children from another marriage, and the stepson of my Uncle Wo Wo.

Ralphie had an unbelievable singing voice and a promising career as an entertainer; however, heroine got the best of him. It was so sad for me to see my cousin, who had so much talent, waste his life away on drugs. One day Ralphie disappeared and was never found again. To this day, it pains me to say that I don't know what happened to my cousin.

One day, my friend Michelle and I were walking through the little neighborhood park and spotted a man sitting alone on the park bench. We decided to pool our money together and give this man a total of five dollars, which was all the money we had. I will never forget how happy he was to receive the cash. He was not the only one who felt joy. We both felt so elated by giving to the less fortunate and hoped that he would buy himself a meal. It was at this time that I realized my love for those who had difficult lives, where poverty and addictions were concerned.

The young "gangster" boys in the neighborhood were already on a hardened path and had no conscience for the needs of humanity. Once, as they walked by the small park near the school—their usual path home—they started taunting the same homeless man. One of them decided to reach into his pocket for his cigarette lighter, and another other boy had lighter fluid. The boy with the can of lighter fluid poured it all over the homeless man's head and clothes. The other took out his cigarette lighter and moved closer tormenting the man with the flame. The boy with the lighter finally threw it on the homeless man, and as the defenseless man's body became engulfed in flames, he burned to death.

The kids were later heard laughing about it to some of their classmates. Some of the kids that overheard this abhorrent story went to the school's superiors and told them what had happened. The boys who committed this horrific crime were arrested and spent much of their time in juvenile hall until they were old enough to stand trial as an adult.

Due to this tragic event, I became keenly aware of the need to help others who were less fortunate and who had faced struggles daily. I had a hard time seeing injustices and cruelty to animals was no different to me than bullying the defenseless people on the streets.

One afternoon I saw a kid in my building kicking a pigeon like a football. I literally screamed at him to stop hurting the bird from my bedroom window. I pushed the window so hard to open it that my hand punched through the glass, slicing my arm. I started bleeding all over my bedroom pillow. I was in terrible pain and didn't know if I damaged a major artery, by the amount of blood I was losing.

Elaine Gordon

My mother and my best friend, Karen, were at my house and grabbed a towel and wrapped my arm. Mom took me straight to the emergency room where I was given seven stitches on my forearm. It was a long laceration and the doctor had a difficult time sewing it up. Today I have a very large scar to remind me that animals need our help too.

Unbroken Vessel

Elaine Gordon

Swapping Places

Marie, "Wash" as she was nicknamed, was one of my mother's best friends who also lived in SoHo. Her apartment, which was one of the nicer tenement buildings, became my second residence. I admired Marie because she was strong and confident. My brother and I were very close to her two children, Artie and Michelle. Artie would spend many weekends at my house playing his electric guitar all day until we fell asleep at night. Today, he is a top-notch lead guitarist in NYC and has dedicated his whole life to music. Interestingly, my brother is also a jazz musician now, and he would love to play saxophone late into the night as well.

I remember one snowy New Year's Eve, my brother and his friend Rubin played their trumpets to serenade the tenants in the building and ring in the New Year. They continued to play well after the bewitching hour of midnight until one of the tenants threw a bag of garbage out of the tenth-floor window. The guys got the message to finish up their set and call it an evening.

The weekends that Artie spent the night at my house, I would stay at his parent's house in the village. My friends and I spent many hours over at Marie's house. She would also hold card games in Brooklyn all night and return home to her apartment early Saturday morning. This was her "job," much like my mother, Marie.

Marie (Wash) would sometimes join in the games and play cards, but her main responsibility was to cook for the other players who would take part in the poker games all night. This is also how she made her money.

In respect and appreciation for staying at her home, I would get up very early on Saturday morning, and clean her entire apartment. That was definitely her love language and I discovered that I really liked to clean houses. Looking back over all these years, little did I know that one day I would own and operate the biggest house-cleaning service in Ft. Lauderdale, Florida, and Seattle, Washington, for over 35 years.

Marie and I became very close, and I truly felt that I had a second mother who balanced me and gave me the security of knowing that she would always be there for me. She was tough on me in a loving way, and I didn't want to disappoint her. When I came home too late from a party and didn't clean up the apartment, I would be awakened by the vacuum cleaner bumping into my bed. It was Marie's way of letting me know that I did not handle my responsibilities of cleaning up the house before she returned. I liked having two places to live in, and although Marie's family was far from perfect, she gave me the sense that everything in my life would be all right.

Marie was married to Artie Sr., a very kind-hearted, loving man that was always gentle to me. Despite working as a bartender and having an alcohol problem, he was very responsible and loved his family.

Marie was the strength of the family, even though she had a boyfriend on the side. Everyone knew the arrangements and although this is not your typical marital situation, I remember that there was always peace and harmony in her home. I know that Artie Jr. would have preferred to have his mother home more often. But, he took comfort in staying at my house on weekends. Artie would always say that he liked the fact that my mom, despite all of her problems, was always home. I found joy in the fact that Artie and I were able to have our needs met by swapping families.

Life moved forward and many of us were now getting ready to graduate from high school. I had just met my first boyfriend in my senior year of high school. His name was Nicky, however many of the kids in the neighborhood called him Sputzy. I could never figure out why so many people in the Italian neighborhood had nicknames— it was part of the Italian culture.

Sputzy was a kind, soft-spoken young man and I enjoyed when he picked me up after school because many of the girls would look out the window and wonder whom the good-looking guy was. I was happy to let them all know that he was my boyfriend. As time moved forward, my boyfriend and I eventually grew apart as my life took on a different direction.

I worked all summer in an Italian restaurant called "Arturo's" on Houston Street, to make enough money to take a trip back to Puerto Rico. I had visited the island with my friend, Michelle, a year earlier and we spent time in San Juan and in Ponce, the second largest city in Puerto Rico. Before the end of the summer, I decided to take the money that I had saved and spent three weeks in Puerto Rico, by myself. I was still only sixteen years old, but I felt like I was mature enough to go on this trip alone.

I met up with friends in San Juan from my last trip to the island who were so gracious to house me for the entire time I was there. They owned a condo on the beach and worked for the airlines.

One of my friends was a pilot, and the other was a flight attendant. Working for the airlines has been a dream of mine since I was ten years old, and this gave me a chance to witness what life was like working for an airline carrier. This sparked my desire even more. I enjoyed flying with them to St. John and St. Thomas, and even had the opportunity to meet the famous rock star, Alice Cooper, sharing a meal with him and his band.

I was reading a magazine one afternoon and came across an advertisement for a school in New York City's Park Avenue area. It was a finishing school called Grace Downs Finishing School, specializing in "Air Career, Business, and Modeling." I thought it couldn't hurt a girl who grew up in the projects to learn how to become refined and polished like in the movie "My Fair Lady."

I inquired about the school, however, the cost was pricey. I began wondering if I could find my father, and perhaps he would support my desire to attend Grace Downs Finishing School.

Through inquiring amongst my father's aunts, Terry and Jo, I located my father. I was so happy to have finally found him, and he agreed to pay for my school. I felt fortunate to be one of the only girls in the welfare housing projects, still living on public assistance, to go to finishing school. This was definitely a first in my neighborhood.

While I contemplated my next move, my brother stayed busy in school and played basketball day and night. He was one of the best players around. Unfortunately, what he lacked was height. When he got accepted into Rice High School, a Roman Catholic college preparatory high school located in Harlem, he was rejected on the basketball team, probably due to his stature. They chose a friend of my brother's, Larry, instead. He was over six-and-a-half feet tall, but he was athletically awkward, could barely dribble a basketball, and my brother demolished him in every game they ever played together.

This affected my brother greatly, especially during tryouts in his second year of high school.

In his sophomore year of high school, he decided to drop out because he didn't have my homework to copy, and had no clue how to study anything but music. When he heard he could drop out at 16 years old, he quit and went to work to make money for our family.

Shortly thereafter he got involved with the wrong crowd and starting experimenting with drugs. He was never a hard-core addict but patiently waited for every payday so he could get high for a few days. Even though he visited the pawnshop occasionally for money, he always went back and retrieved his items, including his beloved saxophone. He once said to me, "If it wasn't for music, I never would have survived. It's what saved my life."

I am glad that he was able to get off hard drugs later in life and make a good life for himself. Many of our friends in the projects died of drug overdoses in their late teens and 20s, and I am grateful to God that my brother was not one of them.

After registering for my finishing school uptown, the feeling of elation filled my being. I felt as though I had a chance in life to make something of myself. Becoming a flight attendant was a career that would give me the opportunity to travel the world, which was always my deepest desire. I would develop a new network of friends that would open up my sphere of influence, globally.

College was never suggested to me, nor was it ever an option. My hunger for self-education was ravenous. I was grateful that I had a chance to attend one of the top finishing schools in New York City. Life was finally looking promising for me, as I was embarking on a brand-new adventure. It all started on Park Avenue.

Elaine Gordon

Welfare Projects to Finishing School

Upon graduation from St. Alphonsus Catholic High School, I spent summers swimming with friends at Pitt Street swimming pool and began preparing for finishing school, which would start in September. I was anticipating all the new adventures I would have, along with meeting new friends. I could not wait until the summer was over, and one month before school started, I received my uniforms in the mail. They were similar to flight attendants' apparel. The school sent two, which gave me some variety in choosing.

School was finally starting in September and the night before I could hardly sleep. I still had to take a bus and subway to school and had to walk quite a distance to reach the school on Park Avenue and 42nd Street. The bus would drop me off on 14th Street, and then I would take the subway train to 42nd Street and 8th Avenue. I did not particularly like walking from 8th Avenue all the way down to Park Ave because I had to walk past many of the X-rated clubs and the off-Broadway Theater District on 42nd Street where hustlers, drug addicts, and prostitutes hung out.

I always managed to walk quickly and arrive at school early. The first day I was so elated to finally step foot into the Pan Am Building, which was across the street from Grand Central Station. As I made my way to my classroom, I was delighted to meet my new classmates. Many of the girls were from different areas in NYC. My new friend, Donna, was from Queens and her parents had a vacation place in the Hamptons, a very affluent and popular summer vacation spot for many successful New Yorker's.

My other good friend, Marsha, was from an area called Hastings-On-Hudson in New York. It overlooked the Hudson River and was about 20 minutes north of midtown Manhattan. One of the other girls in my class was the daughter of a Nicaraguan Ambassador. It was so inspiring to meet young people who aspired to truly make a difference in life.

To my surprise, my new classmates nominated me class President. I could hardly believe my peers nominated me for such a prestigious position. In my former school, I was not one of the most popular girls in the class, probably because my father was not in the Mafia. This school was different. I had a chance to be myself and make friends without any pre-judgments. I spent a lot of time with my new friends and enjoyed many summers at South Hampton Beach.

I was an A+ student moving towards a 4.0 until my modeling teacher said she would not give me an A unless I learned how to walk correctly. My walk was equated to a gangster's walk moving towards a rival gang member preparing for a brawl. I had to spend countless hours on the runway to learn how to balance books on my head without dropping them as I navigated my way across the stage.

My classmates would laugh with me and it took me months to get my flawless walk finally down. I received an A in the class. I believe my modeling teacher felt sorry for me because I worked so hard to walk like a lady, but never did as well as the others. I was satisfied with this because I didn't want to lose my edge being a girl from the hood, and at the same time become an elegant young woman who would be graduating from a school on Park Avenue.

One of the other classes that I loved besides my air career was English class. I had a wonderful English teacher who was enamored with Ernest Hemingway's writings. He noticed that I had a love for words and writing and motivated me to develop my skills. I never realized at the time how much my writing would come into play as my life progressed forward. I am grateful to my teacher for sparking an area of my life that would blaze in years to come.

There was also a significant person in my life that actually fed me throughout my entire year at finishing school. His name was Mr. Frank Calderone, and he worked at the now-defunct automat restaurant next door to my school. He took care of my lunches every day, and I am grateful to him for being one of the angels in my life. It was a privilege getting to know him. His son, Vinny, was a great friend of our family and we considered him one of the closest people in our lives. Even though at times I found life challenging, I was blessed growing up with wonderful people in my life.

I always had God's hand on me, no matter how good or how difficult life was. I knew that I got my strength and will to go on from God, and from the folks in my life who loved and cared for me. To this day, these are the things I think about when I get discouraged and want to give up. I cannot let myself down, let alone anyone else who has invested in me.

That year was the best of my life. Upon graduating from finishing school, I applied for many flight attendant positions, only to find out that I was too young to be hired at 17 years old. Most of the airlines' age requirements for hiring flight attendants were 19 through 21. I was extremely discouraged and decided to look for employment in the city while waiting to become of age to reapply for the position of my dreams.

Unbroken Vessel

Elaine Gordon

Chapter 7

An Entrepreneurial Classroom

My first full-time job, at age 17, was in the largest and most well-known hair salon in the East Village. Around the corner was the Fillmore East, a live theater where I was fortunate enough to see one of Elton John's first concert tours. I fell in love with his music immediately and enjoyed many of the other performers at the time, like Janis Joplin, The Who, and The Beatles.

The hair salon, named Paul McGregor's after the owner, was the most exciting place to work in Manhattan. The salon employed 50 hairstylists and was set up in a factory-style environment.

I was in charge of the front desk, booking all of the appointments, taking payments and administrating the business. I was very good at the business side of things, and selling haircuts was easy for me.

One Saturday afternoon, I challenged myself to fill up every spot on the appointment book. The salon could manage quite a number of clients on Saturdays, and on this particular day, I made a bet with my boss that I would book every appointment slot available. At the end of the day, I was able to book 300 appointments, and it was very exciting to see so many people in the shop. What I did not realize at the time was that this particular business model would be the template I would use for the business that I would open years later. I loved business and somehow had a natural gift of being an entrepreneur. Some people were natural born singers … I had a talent for developing businesses.

My life at this time became very divergent. It was a time when I became much more liberal in my thinking and started hanging around with many people who were much older than I. I was maturing rapidly and somehow lost more of my innocence than I had in Catholic high school. Although I acted older and hung out with people 10 to 15 years my senior, I didn't think about the fact that I was only 17 years old.

I had many new friends from all walks of life and developed friendships with two girls at work named Gracie and Mo. I had never had much experience with motorcycle gangs, except for the Hell's Angels that had one of their clubs only a few blocks away from the projects at 77 E. 3rd Street. I remember walking past their clubhouse hoping no one was sitting outside. It was a scary block to walk down because of their bad reputation.

That was my only experience with the notorious motorcycle gang until I started hanging out with my two girlfriends from work. They both lived in the Bronx and they hung around a motorcycle gang called the "Outlaws." I was not aware that they were just as dangerous as the Hell's Angels because they were very nice to me.

One evening, we were all hanging out in a club in the Bronx when one of the gang members decided to pick a fight with someone at the bar. The place erupted into a large brawl, and most of the place got destroyed in the altercation.

After that, I decided to keep my friendships with these two girls, but only hang out with them at work, because that was more violence than I wanted to witness. Instead, I started going out with some of my other co-workers who hung out in the gay bars in New York's Uptown area. At least those places were not violent, and they had great dance music to move to, and I loved dancing.

I worked in the hair salon for about a year and a half, and during that time I met my boyfriend, Kenny. I instantly fell in love and started dating him. Sadly for me, I did not realize that he was married and had three children. Being so young and impressionable, this was one of the hardest times in my life.

A short while later, I found myself pregnant and I was still only 17 years old. New York State was one of the second states in the country to permit abortion. The law also stated that I did not have to obtain parental consent. I decided to go through with it, but I was apprehensive to tell anyone out of fear. This was extremely difficult for me to handle all by myself, and when I finally told my mother that I had an abortion, she cried and said that she would have been there to support me if she had been able. I loved mom, but at this stage in her life, she was not well enough to help me. I appreciated her heart and how much she loved and cared about me, however, I had to make my own decisions because I was the only one who could take care of me.

Of course, I would have preferred not to have an abortion, but at the time, I had no information or help regarding my situation as this was before the Roe vs. Wade decision by the Supreme Court in 1973. It would have helped to have had some guidance, but now I understand my thinking in making this decision. I reacted out of desperation, fear and impulsive behavior, which led to poor planning. At 17, my brain was still maturing especially in the area known as the "prefrontal cortex." Experts have discovered, that in this area of the brain, we are not quite able to assess risk, think ahead, regulate our emotions, and evaluate ourselves. Although it might seem as though a person 18-25 years old is fully mature, that is not the case for everyone. I regretfully admit, at that time, those functions were definitely not fully developed in me.

In my search for support and true guidance, there was really no one there I could confide in and discuss my situation. I felt isolated and alone and despondent. If I could rewrite history, this would be the one area of my life I would have made a better choice. Remembering times such as these humbles me, and I'm thankful to God for his mercy and forgiveness. I've had to live with the grief-stricken choices I have made. It's only by God's grace that I am able to look myself in the mirror and accept and forgive those decisions and feel good about who I am today.

Elaine Gordon

South Florida via Greenwich Village

Moving from the projects was a decision I encouraged my mother to make because I thought she would like to live in a beautiful apartment back in her Italian neighborhood, to start a new stage in her life. It was the neighborhood where my mother was born and raised and lived most of her unmarried life. She had family and friends still living there, and she was familiar with many of the shop owners on the block.

After moving to our new apartment in SoHo, and leaving our place in the projects after seventeen years, it didn't occur to me that she would have difficulty being on the 6th floor of her new apartment. Mom struggled with walking due to her emphysema and she had become claustrophobic. Taking the elevator was not a good option. As her illness restricted her from going out, she felt isolated and became more depressed as she felt trapped inside of her new dwelling.

Elaine Gordon

I felt the burden of having encouraged her to move from our building where she felt so comfortable and familiar, to a nicer apartment back in her neighborhood. I thought that spending time with her family and old friends would make her life complete and bring her immeasurable joy. That was not the case for my mother.

I never realized that she was happy where we lived before. Our apartment was on the ground floor, back in the projects, and it was easy for her to go outside of the building and chat with the neighbors. In her new place, very few people came to visit her. This is one of those decisions that I wished an adult had helped me make, although my idea was well intended. I also helped her with the rent and many of the utilities to make it easier for her. My mother miserably continued drinking and fell deeper into her depression.

Although it was painful for me, I had to look for a different life for myself. It was not that I did not love her; to the contrary, I had the drive to create a life of my own and become successful in a career so that I could take care of her.

That year, one of my friends, Joey, whom I had grown up with in the projects and was like a brother to me, was heading down to Miami and invited me to go along. I decided I needed a break from work, and the weather in Florida was a stark contrast to the frigid temperatures in New York.

We left several days later and stayed in an area in North Miami Beach on the water, in a motel called the Waikiki, which was located on "Motel Row," The Waikiki was charming and had all of the amenities of a larger hotel but was a fraction of the cost. The weather was warm and lovely, and the salt air was therapeutic. I felt at home on the beach and my desire was to move out of New York City and find a warmer climate, like Miami, in which to reside.

One day, as I was relaxing on one of the lounge chairs facing the ocean's view, I spotted a handsome young man that caught my eye. He had long flowing blond hair, blue eyes, and his skin was golden brown from the sun. He wore a bandana across his forehead, and I could not turn my eyes away. He was a beautiful specimen of a man named Wayne. I spent the weeklong vacation with my friend, Joey, and my new friend, Wayne.

As the days passed, Wayne and I grew closer. When it was time to go home, Wayne asked if I could stay a few more days. I agreed to spend a few more days, knowing that I had an extra week's vacation from work. My good friend Joey needed to return to his job.

In the days that followed, Wayne introduced me to his mother and stepfather, along with his siblings, Lori and Jeff. His family was extremely cordial and had moved from Brooklyn to South

Florida for a better environment for their family. They also had a difficult time coping with the harsh winters on the east coast, and Florida seemed to be the place where many people from New York City were settling.

The day finally arrived when I needed to return to New York City, and I learned that my mother was back in the hospital. I was anxious to see if she was all right. I flew home and headed straight for the hospital.

My mother did not look as well as she normally did. During her hospital stay, I mentioned to her that when she was well enough and was released from the hospital that I would take her to South Florida to meet Wayne. I informed her that I thought it would be good for both of us to move there where the weather was nicer for her to enjoy the outdoors. Although she was extremely weak, she was excited about the possibility of seeing South Florida and spending time with me near the ocean.

After my mother was released from the hospital she was coughing up blood pretty regularly. One of her best friends, Winnie, insisted that she come to live with her in her home so she could care for her properly. Winnie was a lovely woman and a great friend to our family.

My brother, who was also living in our apartment on Sullivan Street, asked if he could temporarily move out and into our Uncle Wo Wo's apartment in the same neighborhood. Uncle Wo Wo allowed this without hesitation as he enjoyed having my brother around.

This meant that I was the only one left in the apartment. I suddenly realize that my little family had been separated and was living in different places. I liquidated the apartment, which was very hard for me to do and moved in with Marie "Wash."

I was now 18, an adult by New York law, so I decided to move to South Florida and join Wayne and his family and make my life in the tropics. We fell in love and decided to get married. We rented a quaint place across the street from the beach. Wayne worked in the film industry as a gaffer for many years. On his off time, he worked at a hotel near the beach, tending to the guests out on the pool deck.

I could hardly wait to relocate my mother so that she could enjoy the beauty of South Florida, the warm ocean breezes, and the fragrance of its tropical environment. I knew that this type of life would be so beneficial for her health. I also missed my mom, and I wanted her to know that I would always be there to help take care of her.

Elaine Gordon

Mourning Mom

Life in Florida's North Miami Beach was quite a change from the life I was accustomed to in New York City. I enjoyed the weather and living across the street from the Ocean. The lifestyle was considerably slower than the pace in the city and I was attracted to the serene culture in Florida.

Wayne and I got along well and as we moved closer towards marriage, I became aware of his daily drinking habits. For some reason, I had many people in my life that had struggled with alcohol. I seemed to drift towards people with the same problems that I was familiar with growing up. I had to work very hard in my life to get to the point of making better choices concerning the people I was involved with. It took many years to learn to be conscious and observe the red flags.

I started looking for employment and took on several jobs as a waitress. I always looked young for my age, and at the age of 18,

I looked as though I was a 14-year-old runaway who left home looking for adventure. I did manage to land two waitress jobs. One of them was located in a fancy hotel on the A1A's Coastal Highway and beach. I worked the breakfast shift in a busy café. Luckily, I had some waitressing experience after I graduated high school when I worked at Arturo's Italian Restaurant in New York. I enjoyed working in a restaurant and serving the public.

The second job I found was at a place located on the Coastal Highway as well. This particular restaurant was named "Lums" and was an upscale hot dog and hamburger place. One afternoon, the manager asked me to work the grill. I had never cooked professionally before, but I flipped and cooked like a pro. Grilling hamburgers, hotdogs, and whatever else customers wanted, I kept the pace in a timely manner.

I didn't mind working in restaurants, but standing over a sizzling grill all day made my clothes and body smell like barbecue. It was not the job I had in mind. It only lasted a short while when another job opened up for me at another hotel. It was the same hotel where Wayne worked, and it included laying cushions over the chase lounges around the pool. I also worked at the pool snack bar serving beer, wine, and fancy drinks.

One afternoon working at the pool shack, Wayne came in late for work. I later discovered that he had been drinking all morning, and had managed to drink two six-packs of beer before one o'clock. I was enraged with his behavior, and we got into a spirited argument. As I walked away, he grabbed me and punched me in the face. My head hit the brick wall inside the pool shack. Blood ran down my face and covered my white bathing suit. The force of his punch broke my nose and almost caused me to blackout.

A few of the guests heard the commotion and ran to bring towels for the blood running down my body. They telephoned emergency assistance, and medics came to help and bandage my nose. One of my friends took me home to rest and put ice packs on my face.

I realized that this was not a healthy relationship. My nature to forgive had no stop signs. Despite the atrocities I endured, I needed to address the physical and mental abuse. It was not okay to allow anyone to violate me in any form of abuse, even if they were remorseful. Forgiveness is one thing, but so are boundaries.

I know, now, relationships must have boundaries. No longer will I surrender to abuse. But as the years followed, it would take many more lessons to learn this reality. As a young girl, my idealism overwhelmed my good senses. Many lessons took years to learn.

Forgiving my mother in most of our violent escapades taught me that forgiving someone who violated me was the right thing to do. I was so wrong in that regard, only because I was so young and innocently naive.

I needed to have healthy boundaries in place to protect myself. Unfortunately, I learned the hard way, which was by trial and error. My determination to set healthy barriers for myself took years of practice. You only know the things that you are subjected to. It was not until others entered my life, as I got older, did I realize this. They enlightened me about such unacceptable behavior so that I could make positive changes. This compelled and drove me to learn how to turn my life around by using my voice and no longer accepting any violations.

Wayne was extremely remorseful the following morning, as many abusers are after an altercation. It took me a while to feel safe again, and I started thinking about returning to NYC.

One late afternoon, as I was at Wayne's mother's house, his mom, Delores, received a phone call from the hospital where my mother was being cared for. I happened to be sitting outside when suddenly Wayne and his mother came outside with somber faces. I knew something was not right, just by their facial expressions. In hushed tones, they said, "Your mother has just died." The news escalated in my ears, getting louder with each beat of my pulse. I felt as though my heart was imploding. I wanted to deny what I was hearing because mom was frequently in and out of the hospitals and she always bounced back.

I had visited her in the hospital just a few weeks earlier and mentioned to her that I wanted her to come to Florida and live with me. "I will take care of you, mom," I promised. That would never happen now. I felt torn up, detached and cried for hours. I wore myself out with tears. Several of my uncles called me from New York and mentioned that they would handle all the arrangements for my mother's funeral.

Wayne and I were given an airline ticket from his mother to fly to New York for the funeral. I did not have very much money and was not sure how to handle the situation. Much of the responsibility fell on me, and mom's passing was a lot to handle for an 18-year-old. My uncles helped because it was their sister, but as sad as all this was, they never asked my brother and me if we needed anything. The uncles that were still alive then were sadly very into their own lives, and the relatives who were good people and really cared about my brother and I were already gone.

The death of my mother overshadowed the violence in my life with Wayne, as we flew to New York so that I could say my last goodbyes. I often felt that if I had been there with her she would have had my support and encouragement to make it through. I felt that she passed away, not only from her illnesses and addictions but also from a broken heart. I felt so guilty about not being there with her as she lay, dying. The thought of my mom dying all alone is more than any individual should have to bear. Her passing at 42-years-old still haunts me. Had I received a phone call to let me know about her critical condition, I would have made provisions to fly to New York and be with her.

I had to handle the affairs of my mother's eternal rest like choosing her burial clothes, and I had to liquidate her small possessions. My brother and I were now truly alone, without any other family involved in our lives. Grandma and my favorite Uncle Benny had died along with Herbie and Aunt Grace—all within the span of a few years, by the time mom died.

My father was somewhere in the world, thousands of miles away. I had no idea how to contact him. I was distraught and in a state of shock, but I always knew God was with me. I reflected on the conversations I had with Him when I was only seven years old, and that always brought me comfort and peace, giving me hope and a promise for the future. That is what my mother would have wanted for me.

There is so much in life that is out of our control. I came to understand that difficulties and hardships, such as dying, are natural sequences in the cycle of life. That doesn't make losing someone you love, any easier. Yet, it helped me become more empathetic and compassionate in my own life, and sympathetic to others in life. Through losing my mom, I learned so much more about handling the trial phases on earth, and that's what caused me to become a stronger and much wiser individual.

Elaine Gordon

Morning Birth

Days after my mother's funeral and burial, Wayne and I headed back to Florida to resume life in our little efficiency apartment in North Miami Beach. We both continued to work at the pool shack and Wayne would intermittently work on various T.V. commercials that came into town. Besides working on the wiring that is used on movie sets, he was also responsible for the execution and sometimes the design of the lighting for films.

My situation at home with Wayne was getting better and his drinking was slowing down. That made it easier for me to get through my mourning period and start to pick up the pieces of my life. I didn't hear from any of my relatives and my brother was dealing with his own personal struggles, as he was rehabilitating from his problem with heroin.

Life appeared quite dark for me at this time, and to help, Wayne brought home a new rescue puppy that was a poodle mix. Naturally, he named the dog "Budweiser." The black puppy cheered me up and I began to feel alive again.

I contemplated what I would do with the rest of my life. Speaking to a friend of my mother's, who was a police officer, gave me great insight. For the first time, I thought about becoming a police officer. The requirements throughout the country were changing and now it was possible for women to become officers. I was still not old enough to become a flight attendant and having a career as an officer would give me stability and room for advancement.

When Wayne came home from work that evening, I mentioned to him what I was thinking. His response really disturbed me. He replied loudly, "If you become a cop, don't let the door hit you in the back." He was essentially letting me know that if I chose the career of a peace officer, I would have to leave my home. Comments like those ran through my body like a bolt of lightning. I had to rethink what I was going to do with my life moving forward. I did not want to be in a relationship with someone that was both physically and verbally abusive. I wanted more for my life.

Several months later, I was feeling less depressed about losing my mom, although there would always be a void in my heart. My mother and I had great difficulties getting along, but we were each other's best friends. Before my mother died, she gave up her drinking and she was lovely to be around. She was soft and gentle and gave me love that I never had. I miss her every day. She taught me how to care for people unconditionally, sometimes to my own detriment. She also taught me how to persevere through the toughest times. I was grateful to her because she was the only person that believed in me and gave me the confidence and fortitude to move forward, by never giving up. Her words sustained me on a daily basis.

In the next weeks to come, I felt very ill and didn't understand what was happening. I was exhausted and was vomiting all the time. This went on for months until one day Wayne rushed me to the hospital. After a series of tests, the doctor came in to speak with me. I was apprehensive and anxious to know his prognosis. "Miss Elaine Mileti," as he referred to me, "I have news for you. You are pregnant and going to have a baby." I was stunned, because during my 19 years I had never any experience with young babies, let alone caring for an infant. Knowing so little, I felt ill-equipped to raise a baby for the first time.

Wayne was very excited about the pregnancy along with the rest of his family. We didn't have much money and lived in a small apartment. Our living room doubled as our bedroom, with one small bathroom and a kitchen all in the same room. The efficiency apartment was 700-square-feet and was definitely not suitable for child rearing.

I had to continue accepting public assistance, which I preferred not to be on. Being on welfare most of my life, I worked hard to show myself that I was an able-bodied adult who could provide for herself without any help from the government's welfare system.

I wanted financial assistance to be available for people who were not able to work due to an illness or a disabling condition. Unfortunately, my mother was very ill most of her life, and desired to work but was unable to pass a board of health test for employment. I remember when the Department of Health and Human Services' Inspectors would visit our apartment. He'd ask mom if she needed anything for my brother and me. She would always reply with a thankful spirit and let the investigator know that we had all we needed.

She would graciously turn down any extra help and thank the person for everything DHHS did for us. My mother did not want to be on public assistance, but as a single mother, and being extremely ill the majority of the time, she asked for as little as possible.

The inspector noticed as he checked through the house that we did not have sufficient winter coats, and we were lacking a bed for myself. I shared a bed with my mother into my early teens as we had a small two-bedroom apartment, and my brother had the other bedroom. I was never ashamed of my poverty. I knew you had to become a hard worker and get an education to escape this lifestyle.

Now, I was an unmarried, pregnant teenager who did not have a college education. I was far from financially able to support a newborn child and myself. Wayne did not make very much money. He made decent money when the film industry jobs came to town, however, that was not very often. He worked at many low-entry jobs and paid for some of our food and bills. However, the majority of his money was spent on drinking with his friends. His mother was a kind-hearted woman and helped us out quite a bit. I felt trapped and isolated—my mother was gone, and my father was nowhere to be found.

I decided to do whatever I needed to do to help support myself and my unborn child. I stocked grocery shelves and started collecting baby clothes from a few garage sales. Although I often wished that I had parents and the guidance of a father, I realized that having a mom and dad in my life was not a reality, so I did the best I could in preparing myself to become a loving, responsible mother. I was determined to be a good mother who cared for her baby and worked hard to provide a happy life. I knew I could not depend on Wayne because he had his own problems with alcohol and eventually drugs, which I later discovered.

One afternoon, I was very hungry and there was not enough food in the house. I discovered a plantain tree outside between my neighbor's house and our apartment. There were several plantains on the tree, so I decided to go over to it and cut them all off so I would have enough to eat. A few hours later, I heard a strange knock at the front door. Standing there was a young woman who looked irritated and unhappy. I asked her what she wanted. She asked, "Did you steal the plantains that I cultivated for the past year?" I was embarrassed, not realizing the tree was someone else's and not to be shared without permission. In my ravenous condition, I hadn't even given it a thought.

I made my apologies and replaced the plantains with a few from the local grocery store. She was unforgiving. She was anticipating fresh plantains grown and nurtured by her. To her annoyance, I assured her that she had done a great job and that they were delicious. I hugged her and thanked her for feeding a neighbor who was pregnant and hungry. From that day forward, Lynn and I became best friends. Who would have thought, that taking my neighbor's plantains, would have brought such a wonderful person into my world!

I didn't show signs of being pregnant for the first six months, but as time flew by, I started to show. I was very thin and only gained 20 pounds during the nine months of my pregnancy. One early evening, two weeks into my ninth month, I started feeling strong pains in my lower back. I did not realize my labor was beginning. Wayne drove me to the hospital, dropped me off, and left to look for his friends to celebrate the birth of his child.

Meanwhile, I suffered with labor pains for 24 hours straight. The hospital I was in did not believe in giving anything to relieve pain during labor. It was an Osteopathic Hospital and when I was ready to deliver, a day later, they finally gave me what was called a saddle block. The anesthesiologist numbed my body from the waist down finally giving me relief for the first time in more than 24 hours. I had cried and screamed during the pain, as being alone during the birth of my first child was scary and hard without my mother by my side.

Wayne finally made it back to the hospital and was able to stay with me during the final stages of my labor and during the birth of our first child. The doctor was already in the operating room and waiting for the nurses to wheel me in to deliver my baby. I was so happy and frightened at the same time. About thirty minutes later, my beautiful baby daughter Shavawn was born at 12:12 a.m.

Humorous as this was, she actually sounded like a duck after she made her entrance into the world to take her first breath. She was a tiny baby, weighing only 5 pounds, 15 ounces. She was so beautiful— totally bald with large brown eyes that sparkled, still present today.

At that moment, I knew what love was all about. I've never experienced such a love as giving birth to your own child. I can understand, now, how and why my mother loved me so much. Mom always said I would give birth to a daughter just like me. I never fully understood what she meant by that until I had my own daughter. Then, I understood what my mother meant as my own daughter started growing up herself.

Even at birth, I knew she was destined to be independent and strong in nature. I knew that I had to cultivate a good-hearted, loving nature in Shavawn, just as my mother had in me.

After my daughter's birth, I realized what my responsibilities were in raising my daughter. I wanted an atmosphere that would be easier for her than the home life I was subjected to as a child.

At times, we witness the cycles of life and observe its adversities, whether by our own choices or by fate. We must discover the silver linings in life's challenging lessons. These insights, although driven by our hardships, will bring us immeasurable wisdom, strength and the fortitude to pioneer the journey that lies ahead.

In closing, of my first book from a series to be continued about my life, I want to leave you with one final thought: Often times, we are the hardest on ourselves, due to the many failures that we have endured. Failures are truly the prerequisite to success. It is not how many times we have fallen, but instead, it is the determination that motivates us to take a stand. "It is not what happens to us that defines who we are, but rather it is what we do with what happens to us, that defines who we will become."

Elaine Gordon

CONCLUSION

You have finally reached the end of my first book. I hope you, my beautiful reader, have enjoyed my bittersweet journey through the pages of my formative years.

My desire is for you to know that you too—no matter how easy or difficult your life has been—can make a difference in life. The lessons we have learned in our lives can help others navigate through their own difficulties.

I feel that our purpose in life is to contribute something back. In the great words of Mother Teresa, "We ourselves feel that what we are doing is just a drop in the ocean, but the ocean would be less because of that missing drop."

"It is not how much we do, but how much love we put in the doing. It is not how much we give, but how much love we put in the giving."

- Mother Teresa

- Elaine Gordon

Elaine Gordon

AUTHOR'S NOTE

As a Board-Certified Integrative Nutrition Health Coach, I decided to make my specialty—besides the proper nutrition that you ingest—relationship coaching. Relationships are the first "foods" that you feed your body with. This is called one of your "primary foods," which keeps your body sustained in a healthy manner.

Having good relationships are vital to maintain a balance in your life and oftentimes this is one of the most forgotten "food" groups.

Throughout my life, I have struggled with many of my relationships. I realized that in order to work on having healthy relationships, I must work on becoming healthy myself in the primary food category.

Throughout my story, over the first twenty years of my life, I was not raised to understand what a healthy relationship was. My life was chaotic, dysfunctional and without much guidance. I have worked tirelessly cultivating and continuing to strive for healthiness in myself, so that I can recognize that sort of healthiness in others. It has been quite a task to become conscious and aware of what I needed to change in my life to become the person that I was born to be.

I am determined to continue to grow and become the best version of myself. In the next two books that I'm planning to write, I will take you through the difficult challenges I faced getting divorced and raising and supporting my children by myself, while continuing to maintain a positive attitude. I will share the pains and sufferings of raising four children—pregnant, homeschooling, and living homeless for nearly a year, all while being a victim of domestic violence.

I have a passion for life, love and the pursuit of happiness, and I also have a passionate heart to help others, especially those that are less fortunate.

There is so much to be thankful and grateful for in life and what is important is to become a better person, rather than a bitter person. I learned how to extend grace, mercy and forgiveness to all those who have hurt me or caused me harm. I am able to be filled with much joy and love for others and most of all, I am filled with a healthy love for myself.

My message to you, my dear reader, is to look at your life, and although we all have hard times to overcome, there are so many things to be thankful for.

I also want to encourage you to, "Never, Never, Never Give Up," in the wonderful words of Winston Churchill.

And finally, there is always a silver lining in all of our challenges. You just have to be persistent and look inside the cloak you have been given.

Elaine Gordon

ABOUT THE AUTHOR

Elaine Gordon received her education as a Board-Certified Integrative Nutrition Health and Nutritional Coach from the Institute for Integrative Nutrition in NYC. IIN is the largest nutritional school in the world and has a global outreach of over 100,000 students and graduates in over 150 countries. Gordon's specialty, besides nutritional coaching for your bio-individual body and lifestyle, is in the area of the "primary foods" as a relationship coach. Gordon is an ambassador for the Institute for Integrative Nutrition and would be delighted to share more about IIN with you. You can contact her by email at elaine@elainegordonconsulting.com.

Gordon is also a single mother and has supported and raised three successful adult children and two stepchildren, and she also has two grandchildren and two step-grandchildren.

As a professional freelance writer, Gordon has published monthly recipes, featured stories and a monthly column called "Celebrity Eats" for The City Magazine in El Paso, Texas.

As the owner of the only Intraceuticals Oxygen Infusion Beauty Spa in El Paso, Gordon enjoys bringing health and youth to the skin.

Gordon's experience as an entrepreneur started at the age of 19 when she launched Elaine's American Maid in Ft. Lauderdale, Florida and Seattle, Washington. While living in the Seattle area, Gordon started two foundations: "Maid for Work," which launched low-income women into their own successful housecleaning service, and "Maid for Life," which provided free housecleaning for women living with breast cancer, and men whom have lost their wives to cancer. Through these efforts, she has launched at least 5,000 women into their own entrepreneurial businesses for nearly 40 years.

More of Gordon's past work as an entrepreneur includes owning and operating Gordon's Production and Public Relations Firm, producing work that includes a short documentary film, "The Heroes of Ground Zero," which was nominated for an Emmy. Other film projects she has produced include "Silhouettes of Time" which was featured on HBO.

Gordon served on two boards in Washington State: The Washington State Attorney General's Task Force for Domestic Violence and The Traumatic Brain Injury Association following a severe unlimited hydroplane crash that her former husband, Hydroplane Racer Mark Evans, suffered.

Today, Gordon has made her home in El Paso, Texas—one of the world's largest border communities and also home to Ft. Bliss military base.

Gordon is planning to speak across America and globally about domestic violence and abuses with the hope of helping victims overcome their fear and trauma, and to give them hope and encouragement to have an empowered life.

Would you like more copies of
UNBROKEN VESSEL?

For each copy, please send a check or money order for $17.95 US/Can $23.50, plus $3.50 for shipping and handling (US funds), per book to:

Elaine Gordon
5821 Vista Clara Drive
El Paso, Texas. 79912

To order by phone, please have your Visa or MasterCard ready and call 206-409-2133, or leave a message.

For more information on volume discounts, please call 206-409-2133, or email: elaine@elainegordonconsulting.com

Would you like to know more about the Institute for Integrative Nutrition? Please email Elaine Gordon at: elaine@elainegordonconsulting.com

Elaine Gordon

Made in the USA
Lexington, KY
02 November 2019